TRADE SECRETS

A REFERENCE GUIDE TO LEADERSHIP EXCELLENCE

KEVIN J. PETERSON

For permission requests, write to the author, addressed "Attention: Permissions Coordinator," at: tradesecrets2023@gmail.com.

Hardcover ISBN 9798868077630

Paperback ISBN 9798868082009

E-Book Available

Cover Design: Yasir Nadeem

Trade Secrets - A Reference Guide to Leadership Excellence is a work of fiction. Names, characters, businesses, places, events, and incidents are either the products of the author's imagination or used in a fictitious manner. Any resemblance to actual persons, living or dead, or actual events is purely coincidental.

Kevin J. Peterson

DEDICATION

To my cherished wife Trina and my beloved daughter Keely. This book is a testament to the unwavering love, support, and inspiration you both have infused into every chapter of my life. Trina, your strength, grace, and enduring partnership are the foundation upon which I build my dreams. Keely, your youthful curiosity and boundless imagination remind me that magic and wonder are always within reach.

Keely, as you embark on your pursuits, may this book be a reminder that curiosity opens doors to endless possibilities, imagination fuels innovation, and aloha and integrity triumph above all else.

This book is dedicated to you, my two pillars of strength and love. May its pages be a small reflection of my gratitude and admiration for you both. Thank you for filling my life with love, laughter, and boundless joy.

With All My Love…

Table of Contents

Preface 1

Introduction 3

SECTION I: Forging the Foundation of Leadership 5

Chapter 1: Leading with Honor 7

Chapter 2: The Authority Advantage 17

Chapter 3: The Power of Grit 33

Chapter 4: Communication: The Make or Break Skill 43

Chapter 5: Decisive Leadership 53

Chapter 6: Leading with Imagination 65

Chapter 7: Adaptability, Toughness, and Problem Solving 77

Chapter 8: Courageous Leadership 87

Chapter 9: Cool, Calm, and Collected Leadership 99

SECTION II: Crafting Your Leadership Style 109

Chapter 10: Leading by Example 111

Chapter 11: Resilience & Thick Skin 121

Chapter 12: Enthusiasm in Leadership 131

Chapter 13: Vigor Unleashed 139

Chapter 14: The Power of Approachability 147

Chapter 15: Leadership in the Age of Empathy 157

Chapter 16: Inspire to Aspire 167

Chapter 17: Leading with Laughter 179

SECTION III: Navigating Leadership Challenges 187

Chapter 18: From Micro to Macro 189

Chapter 19: The Power of Delegation 201

Chapter 20: The Educator's Mission 211

Chapter 21: Leadership through Team Building 221

Chapter 22: The Art of Walking Around 231

Chapter 23: The Science of Time Management 241

SECTION IV: Advanced Leadership Techniques 249

Chapter 24: Kaizen: The Path to Continuous Improvement ... 251

Chapter 25: The Game of Interviewing 259

Chapter 26: Strategic Negotiation 277

Chapter 27: Financial Fluency 289

Conclusion: A Toast to Leadership Excellence 299

Author Biography 305

Kevin J Peterson

PREFACE

Trade Secrets - A Reference Guide to Leadership Excellence is a
compilation of over 300 tips and tricks of the trade gathered throughout
40 years of collaboration with colleagues. Many of these insights were
shared and developed in post-work gatherings, where we unwound from
the day's pressures while engaging in discussions about leadership and
self-improvement, "occasionally" accompanied by a few libations at the
local pub. This often disregarded facet of leadership development
pertains to the significant transformation that unfolds as the workday
comes to an end, affording leaders the chance for self-reflection and
personal growth. These moments allow managers and leaders to step
away from the daily grind, engage in meaningful discussions, and reflect
on their workplace experiences. It is during these informal gatherings
where camaraderie and shared insights flow as freely as the cocktails and
draft beer.

Without the constraints of pressing work-related demands, these after-
hours conversations become a stage for self-examination and
contemplation. Managers and leaders candidly discuss the intricacies of
their roles, share noteworthy stories about their teams and supervisors,
and address the challenges they encounter. In this liberated state, they
passionately pursue personal leadership excellence and the desire to
inspire others with their own leadership qualities. While the workday
may be filled with meetings, deadlines, and unrelenting pressures, it's a
well-established fact that leaders are often at their most authentic during
these relaxed, off-duty moments.

1

Within the pages of this book, you'll find an invaluable resource for aspiring leaders and those looking to enhance their leadership abilities. Each chapter is dedicated to dissecting a specific set of traits necessary for becoming a great leader. But what makes this book truly unique is the way it presents these vital insights. The contents are structured around what I've always endearingly called **"Trade Secrets."** These are not just abstract theories but actionable principles that can be applied immediately to your leadership journey. In each chapter, you'll discover a wealth of actionable guidance presented in the form of Actions, Techniques, and the Benefits they yield. These "Trade Secrets" will be your go-to toolkit for leadership excellence, readily accessible whenever needed. Whether you're a seasoned leader or just starting your leadership adventure, you'll find these insights and strategies to be invaluable resources as you progress on your path to becoming a remarkable leader.

INTRODUCTION

Crafting Your Leadership Legacy

Welcome to *Trade Secrets - A Reference Guide to Leadership Excellence*. Success in the world of careers frequently depends on being an authority in a particular field, mastering a specific discipline, and perfecting your skills. However, a completely different set of principles apply when it comes to leadership.

The profound distinction between succeeding in a specialized career and taking on leadership duties is captured by the adage, "To have a successful career, you must be great at one thing; to be successful as a leader, you must be great at many." You may have established a reputation for being the go-to expert in your field during your career; however, switching to leadership is like entering a brand-new arena.

Leadership requires a broad skill set that goes much beyond one specific area of specialization. It includes the idea of communication, the capacity for making critical judgments, the talent to solve complex issues, the ability to promote teamwork, and the emotional intelligence to bring it all together. Influential leaders are well-balanced individuals who can motivate, direct, and get the best out of others to achieve success for their company and, just as importantly, their team.

Your transformative leadership path is all about creating your personal brand and image. Do You Have a Brand? What Do You Want Your Brand to Be? Every leader needs to strategically develop their individual brand. While seasoned managers may need to polish theirs, new managers are still formulating theirs. In many ways, being a leader is similar to playing a part on the big stage of an organization. However, despite not yet having mastered your role entirely, others have already cast you in the part of an exceptional leader and hold high expectations for your performance.

This book is your guide for developing the vital leadership abilities that will put you on the road to success. You'll learn to "fake it until you make it," even if you're unsure of your leadership skills. As you continue to "fake it," these leadership qualities will increasingly become a part of who you are, defining your brand, your identity, and ultimately your legacy.

"Make a Toast" to the road that lies ahead as you learn how to become a formidable leader, navigate the challenges of human behavior, and eventually leave a lasting impression on your company and career. The time is now to create your leadership legacy.

SECTION I

FORGING THE FOUNDATION OF LEADERSHIP

Welcome to Section I, where the foundation of your leadership identity is established. Just as a talented mixologist painstakingly sources and blends numerous ingredients to produce a masterpiece, we've combined the core principles of great leadership to provide you with the structural integrity upon which to succeed. In this collection of chapters, we will discuss the characteristics of successful leaders: integrity, the cornerstone of leadership; authority, which determines the dynamics of leadership; and resilience and tenacity, which fuel your pursuit of excellence. Our journey will also take us through the benefits of effective communication, the decisiveness required to lead confidently, and the visionary thinking that sparks creativity and innovation. So, join us on this journey as we set the stage for leadership success, raising a glass to your growth and empowerment.

CHAPTER 1

LEADING WITH HONOR:
INTEGRITY AS THE BEDROCK OF LEADERSHIP

In my forty years of negotiating the complex world of business, the importance of integrity has remained constant. They continue to be the unshakable standard of moral leadership, the cornerstone of trust, and the pillar of honor that determines the fate of not only people but entire companies. Unfortunately, in a world where integrity is not always the norm, it is critical that great leaders foster, honor, and demand it as an essential component of our leadership development.

Ethical Leadership: Abraham Lincoln's Legacy

Integrity in the context of leadership goes well beyond following the letter of the law or following company policy. It stands for a fundamental dedication to moral behavior, an uncompromising commitment to upholding morality, and a steadfast determination to create an inspiring example for others to imitate. Uncompromising, moral leaders become beacons of ethical leadership, illuminating the way for their teams with their unbending values.

Let us explore Abraham Lincoln's incredible journey, a historical example of the profound influence of moral leadership. His effect as the 16th President of the United States was not only a result of his high office but also firmly entrenched in his steadfast dedication to morality and justice. President Lincoln showed exceptional integrity by working diligently to abolish slavery and unite the country in the face of the enormous challenges of the American Civil War. His unrelenting commitment to upholding the Union and promoting equality exemplified the true meaning of ethical leadership.

Abraham Lincoln's influence was intricately connected to his moral principles and not just his position as President. He was adamant that upholding ethical principles was necessary, and his actions clearly conveyed that integrity is not just a concept in leadership; it is a way of life, a guiding philosophy that leaders should aspire to in their organizations, their country, and themselves.

The Alignment of Values with Actions

Integrity is more than a phrase or a hollow slogan trumpeted by business titans; it is a daily practice that underpins every decision and activity. It is about connecting one's ideals with one's conduct, especially when faced with the most challenging decisions. In this setting, authority serves as a diligent watchdog, ensuring that certain ethical ideals are followed consistently.

Consider a hotel general manager who is presented with a decision: maximize earnings or fulfill reservations for a relocated family during the busy Christmas season. Because of their dedication to ethics, this manager chooses the latter, even if it means making financial compromises. Such an act has a strong emotional impact on both consumers and workers, supporting the concept that leaders are not only entrusted with authority but also with the ethical obligation to make decisions that are consistent with the values of their business.

Leaders who realize that integrity is a constant commitment rather than a one-time decision motivate their colleagues to do the same. They understand that integrity is more than a checkbox on a corporate ethics form; it is a fundamental and enduring mindset that should guide all aspects of their business operations.

The Courage to Take the High Road

Understandably, it takes enormous courage to uphold values consistently; otherwise, this book would not need to emphasize this attribute. Outstanding leadership is characterized by a deep commitment to supporting moral principles even when compromise is the more straightforward or accessible course of action. Imagine a restaurant manager who steadfastly refuses to serve a meal that does not meet the required quality requirements despite intense pressure from superiors. This selfless deed demonstrates their uncompromising dedication to ethics and refusal to take shortcuts. Leaders with this level of conviction show that integrity is not a matter of convenience; it is about always choosing the high road, even in the face of adversity or temptation.

Embracing Mistakes: The Integrity of Leadership Accountability

Leaders make mistakes, which is an often overlooked fact. Amidst the thousands of decisions made weekly, mistakes and uninformed choices are inevitable. The essence of leadership integrity is not perfection but the ability to confront and correct errors when made.

Leadership integrity shines when leaders humbly admit their mistakes. This starts with taking responsibility and openly admitting when a mistake is made. Rather than ignoring it or blaming someone else, a confident leader accepts responsibility for the decisions made, whether through oversight, poor judgment, or lack of information.

When necessary, apologizing becomes a formidable instrument in the arsenal of a genuine leader. A real admission of faults indicates transparency and honesty, restoring trust and fostering a culture where acknowledging mistakes is considered a strength.

However, the road to redemption does not end with an apology. Whether it is recalibrating a flawed strategy, reevaluating a decision, or implementing changes to prevent recurrence, the willingness to correct is critical. This proactive strategy demonstrates adaptability, resilience, and a commitment to continual progress.

Communication is essential. Leaders must be truthful in their decisions and clear in their resolutions. Sharing the measures used to correct a mistake emphasizes accountability and nurtures the principles of transparency within the team.

In the broad tapestry of leadership, mistakes are not stains but possibilities for progress. Leaders who truly admit, correct, and disclose their mistakes demonstrate a remarkable level of honesty. Leaders establish an environment of trust, resilience, and shared learning by being transparent and committed to continuous development, leading their people to common achievement.

The Convergence of Personal & Professional Integrity

Throughout my tenure in the hospitality sector, I have enjoyed witnessing how strong leaders frequently combine their personal and professional integrity. These leaders interweave their personal principles into their professional sphere, creating a healthy and vibrant environment.

Let's consider the path of Michael, a restaurant owner who is passionate about caring for his neighborhood. In order to balance his personal principles with his professional obligations, Michael makes sure that his business uses locally sourced materials, collaborates with adjacent companies, and actively participates in community programs. When his personal and professional ethics collide, a community-focused dining experience is created that appeals to his customers with similar beliefs. Simultaneously, it inspires his employees, who witness his impact on the community in which they live.

Lack of Integrity: A Costly Lesson in Leadership

Now imagine an example where Dave, a manager with questionable ethics, leads a team at a well-known hotel chain. Dave's management style serves as a stark illustration of the adverse outcomes of a lack of integrity in leadership.

Consider a circumstance involving a workplace harassment complaint that was reported to Dave. Instead of addressing it immediately, Dave made the decision to cover up the problem so the issue, which occurred within his department, would not tarnish his reputation in the eyes of his superiors. Rather than dealing with it appropriately, he instructs the affected staff to remain silent and not to report it to Human Resources.

Dave's secrecy and lack of action only enflame the issues, escalating the problem. As a result, the victims of the harassment feel abandoned and defenseless, employee morale falls to an all-time low, productivity decreases, and ultimately, talented employees leave the company.

The effects of Dave's lack of integrity on the team's chemistry, workplace morale, and overall performance were extensive. It was a costly leadership lesson highlighting how crucial honesty, openness, and moral decision-making are. This case serves as a sobering example of how executives who put themselves first through short-term cover-ups and secrecy above integrity can ultimately harm the prosperity and well-being of their enterprises. On the other hand, leaders who uphold integrity foster loyalty, trust, and long-term success.

Tips & Tricks

1. **Action: Promote "Hypothetical" Ethical Discussions**
   - **Technique**: Create forums where open dialogue about moral dilemmas and difficulties can occur. Encourage your staff to engage in ethical debates and to seek counsel when faced with moral uncertainty. Bring up a hypothetical

situation during team meetings, such as: "A supplier offers a sizable incentive in exchange for a lucrative contract; what do you do?" Encourage your team members to brainstorm and practice ethical arguments and responses.

- **Benefit:** The consideration of ethical principles in decision-making becomes more commonplace by encouraging honest discussions. Actively addressing ethical problems ensures they are not dismissed and helps create a culture of ethical awareness and accountability within your team. These discussions enable your team to forge a shared moral compass, improving their capacity to make good decisions in practical circumstances and reiterating the value of ethical behavior in your business.

2. **Action: Mentorship in Ethics**
   - **Technique:** Share your experiences, moral quandaries, and critical insights with rising team members to help them create a solid ethical foundation. Regular discussions regarding ethical situations provide them with a forum to seek assistance and reflect on their own principles in relation to the company's ethical standards.
   - **Benefit:** Ethics mentoring enables people to establish their own moral compass. It highlights those leaders who place integrity first and those that don't. It also emphasizes the significance of ethical leadership as a pillar of your company's values.

3. **Action: Ethical Recognition**
   - **Technique:** Create a method for your team or organization to acknowledge and celebrate ethical actions. Recognize those who continuously defend moral principles and exhibit integrity.
   - **Benefit:** The public or individual recognition of ethical decision-making reinforces the role of integrity in leadership

and the work environment. It encourages others to follow the same path as they recognize that their actions will be recognized and appreciated. It also establishes a standard for outstanding ethical behavior within the organization.

4. **Action: Respect – Yes, The 'Golden Rule' is Still A Thing**
    *   **Technique:** Respect entails appreciating another person's rights, thoughts, and ideas regardless of upbringing, beliefs, or status. It involves treating people with respect, fairness, and kindness by the Golden Rule, which has been a cornerstone of human behavior for millennia.
    *   **Benefit:** Respect creates a supportive and welcoming workplace. It improves communication, lessens conflict, and promotes a variety of opinions. Respect is a leadership virtue that encourages tolerance and acceptance, strengthening team cohesion creating an environment of decency and mutual regard.

5. **Action: Ethical Decision-Making**
    *   **Technique:** When faced with complex challenges, ethical decision-making entails navigating complex challenges by consistently choosing morally sound courses of action. It involves careful thought of how your actions ripple throughout the workplace and society, with an emphasis on the larger good and long-term consequences.
    *   **Benefit:** Making ethical decisions strengthens your dedication to honesty and moral conduct. It establishes a moral foundation for your leadership, instilling confidence and trust. Additionally, it serves as an example for your team, motivating them to make moral decisions and adopting ethical workplace principles.

6. **Action: The Buck Stops Here**
   - **Technique:** Accountability entails taking responsibility for your actions, including admitting mistakes and taking steps to fix them. It involves taking responsibility for the consequences of your choices. It also entails avoiding "throwing someone under the bus" in order to protect yourself and accepting responsibility even when things go wrong, refraining from placing the blame on others.
   - **Benefit:** Accountability improves transparency and trust in your leadership. It promotes a culture of responsibility among your team members when you act as an example of accountability and refrain from assigning blame. It also indicates your dedication to moral conduct and ongoing development. This strategy not only promotes cohesion and a sense of shared accountability, but it also helps you establish a reputation as a leader who accepts responsibility for their activities, regardless of difficulties or setbacks.

7. **Action: Transparency**
   - **Technique:** Transparency calls for direct and honest communication, ensuring that pertinent information is disclosed, mainly when it affects others. It entails sharing knowledge about decision-making procedures and being honest about goals.
   - **Benefit:** Transparency develops trust and promotes cooperation and openness. Prioritizing openness indicates your dedication to justice and moral behavior. It promotes communication among team members so that decisions may be made with more knowledge.

8. **Action: Simple Honesty**
   - **Technique:** Integrity is a precondition for honesty, which calls for you to always tell the truth, even in trying circumstances. It includes being truthful in your words and

deeds, abstaining from deception, and giving accurate information.

- **Benefit:** Since people can rely on your directness and sincerity, honesty enhances credibility. It encourages an atmosphere of open dialogue where problems can be handled honestly. It also promotes moral conduct throughout the entire corporation.

Chapter Summary

Integrity is the steady guiding light of morality, a necessity for developing trust, and the foundation upon which character is built. Beyond following the rules, ethical leadership entails a firm commitment to decency and a steadfast upholding of moral principles in the face of obstacles or temptations. Integrity-filled leaders become role models for ethical leadership, illuminating the way for their teams with their unwavering values. It takes courage to uphold moral standards, particularly in business, where moral decisions frequently require firm resolution. Integrity should guide every aspect of business operations; it is more than just a box to check on a corporate ethics form. It involves continually balancing one's professional and personal principles and having the guts to follow the correct route, even when it presents additional difficulties. These behaviors support the values of moral leadership and work to create a more ethical present and future for the business sector and beyond.

CHAPTER 2

THE AUTHORITY ADVANTAGE:
SHAPING LEADERSHIP FOR IMPACT

Authority is not merely a role thrust upon a manager; it symbolizes a guiding force, defining a path to achieving organizational objectives and instilling a sense of purpose and accountability within the team. In this chapter, our aim is to gain insights into the complexities of authoritative leadership by examining the tactics and qualities that give leaders their unique edge and ability to lead effectively.

A Leadership Presence

Imagine a leader—not necessarily a CEO—but someone who sets a good example, elevates confidence, and inspires trust. This is the essence of leadership, which is attainable by all. It is not just about titles or positions but also about the ethereal aura that a leader exudes.

Now, let's examine Steve Jobs, who was a co-founder of Apple Inc. His influence was derived from his position as CEO, his unbreakable spirit, and his charismatic vision. His leadership style set the standard for Apple's quality and innovation. The world knew that when they watched Jobs present at the Apple product premieres, sporting his signature black turtleneck, they were watching a leader who radiated authority through his presence and faith in Apple's ground-breaking goods.

Steve Jobs was much more than a CEO; he was a visionary. His leadership power stemmed from his relentless pursuit of greatness. He demonstrated how excellent leadership presence transcends titles, exceeding the bounds of one's position and instilling a profound feeling of purpose, trust, and steadfast faith in the mission at hand in those around them. Jobs' example inspired not only devotion but also a shared dedication to greatness, leaving an indelible effect on both Apple and the world of technology.

The Strategic Alignment with Integrity

Integrity serves as the compass. It drives judgments and behavior. Authority is the guardian that ensures these ideals are faithfully followed.

Take Warren Buffett's career as an investor and CEO of Berkshire Hathaway as an example. His prominence in the financial world results from his enormous wealth and, more significantly, his dedication to ethical investing. Investors from all around the world trusted him because of his commitment to integrity.

A foundation of integrity serves as the basis for Warren Buffett's authority. His commitment to transparent and moral corporate conduct improved his reputation as an individual and established his dominance in the financial industry. His example demonstrates that moral integrity, not just influential power, gives authoritative legitimacy.

The Confidence of a Seasoned Leader

A leader must confidently steer the ship even when storms are approaching. Imagine a business executive with the grace and self-assurance of Indra Nooyi, the former CEO of PepsiCo, navigating the challenges of the beverage and snack industry.

Nooyi's unshakeable confidence was a distinguishing feature that shone brilliantly throughout her distinguished career. She bravely faced many challenges, making an unmistakable impact as one of the world's most prominent female CEOs. Her journey was distinguished by a series of problematic difficulties; each faced with a steadfast will to succeed.

One significant challenge she faced was leading PepsiCo during a period of significant transformation in the beverage and snack industry. Not only did this include managing a diverse and widely dispersed staff, but also adjusting to ever-changing consumer tastes and health-conscious tendencies. Nooyi's belief in her abilities and vision enabled her to face these problems head-on. She was confident in her strategic choices and adaptable enough to the changing market conditions, which proved critical in leading PepsiCo toward long-term growth and success.

Nooyi's leadership experience eloquently demonstrates the power of self-assurance in leadership. It goes beyond her individual accomplishments and demonstrates the transforming power of a leader's confidence and capacity to inspire and guide people through the most difficult conditions.

The Fusion of Personal & Professional Authority

A leader's impact is typically magnified when two diverse types of authority effortlessly converge, as shown by the extraordinary Eleanor Roosevelt. Her life is a vivid example of the unrivaled power of combining personal and professional influence.

Eleanor Roosevelt exhibited extraordinary personal influence that stemmed from her unrelenting commitment to social justice, equality, and human rights. Her dedication to these values not only showed her true character but also provided the groundwork for her influential professional endeavors. Eleanor was not only a supporter of bold ideas; she also possessed the poise and strategic skill to translate those ideals into real, measurable accomplishments. It was her extraordinary capacity to merge her personal and professional impact that catapulted her to unprecedented heights.

Eleanor Roosevelt was instrumental in furthering human rights on a global scale, thanks to the combination of her personal views and professional activities as a diplomat, novelist, and humanitarian. Her influence extended far beyond the confines of any particular function, and she forever changed the role of America's First Lady. Eleanor's leadership abilities extended beyond traditional limits, leaving a legacy that continues to inspire and impact the world. Her singular combination of personal and professional power is an enduring illustration of the incredible heights that leadership may achieve when these two forces combine.

Emotional Intelligence

Emotional intelligence (EI) is the ability to understand, manage, and navigate one's own emotions and the emotions of others effectively. Great leaders recognize the value of EI in exercising power and control. Leaders can use EI to understand and pilot their environment, assist when needed, and motivate staff, regardless of their title or position. To effectively manage leadership issues, great leaders should be aware of numerous idiosyncrasies and undesirable tendencies in human behavior. Among these oddities and habits are:

- **Confirmation Bias:** People often make biased decisions by seeking out information that confirms their beliefs.
- **Groupthink:** Group settings have the tendency to promote conformity, which can put a damper on creativity, critical thinking, and progress.
- **Overconfidence:** People sometimes overestimate their skills and capabilities, which can result in risky and potentially dangerous decisions.
- **Procrastination:** Procrastination or delaying important tasks can lead to reduced productivity and hinder growth.

- **Negativity Bias:** Generally, people have a tendency to recall and fixate on negative experiences more than positive ones.
- **Resistance to Change:** A significant number of people possess a natural inclination towards resisting change, which can make it difficult to introduce and implement new ideas or strategies.
- **Emotional Contagion:** Emotions have the capacity to spread amongst team members, impacting both morale and productivity.
- **Self-Serving Bias:** The emotions of one team member can easily affect the rest of the team, leading to a decrease in morale and productivity.
- **Anchoring:** People often rely heavily on the first piece of information they encounter, affecting judgment and decision-making
- **Social Loafing:** Some individuals will exert less effort in a group, expecting others to compensate.
- **Halo Effect:** Positive qualities in one area do not necessarily mean competence in other areas. This assumption can potentially lead to clouded judgment.
- **Sunk Cost Fallacy:** People may continue committing to a project or decision despite mounting losses.

Great leaders understand the importance of acknowledging the idiosyncrasies and habits of their team members in order to minimize their impact on the team and the organization as a whole. By taking the time to recognize these unique tendencies, leaders can create a more positive and productive work environment for everyone involved.

Knowing When & How to Use Discipline

Discipline awareness is a crucial component of authority in developing leadership abilities. It goes beyond the employment of punitive measures and is best utilized as a tactical tool for promoting good behavioral change within teams and organizations. Influential leaders understand that the importance of knowing when and how to enforce discipline is as crucial as knowing when to offer support and encouragement.

The Delicate Balance

Consider a situation where a team member regularly misses deadlines or behaves disruptively. A compassionate leader knows that solving this problem necessitates striking a careful balance between the "carrot" and the "stick."

Using the "Carrot"

The application of incentives and positive reinforcement is symbolized by the "carrot." Offering incentives, commendations, or opportunities for growth to team members who show improvement-minded behavior can be successful. This approach encourages individuals to perform better by aligning their efforts with the potential achievement of their short-term or long-term personal goals. Understanding the employee's relationship to these short and long-term goals by the leader is imperative when developing such plans.

Using the "Stick"

On the other hand, the "stick" represents the responsible application of reprimand when required. It could be necessary to use sanctions when wrongdoing or poor performance continues despite encouragement and support. However, rather than being used as a means of retaliation or punishment, these consequences should be equitable, consistent, and aimed at helping people change for the better.

Consider a scenario where a team member routinely refuses to follow the organization's rules for professional behavior. In these instances, a leader would respectfully address a team member, employing the "stick" tactic, who would then clearly detail the consequences of their behavior both verbally and in writing. Additional instruction or coaching to address the underlying problems may be one of these results. By doing this, the team leader hopes to make the team members more aware of the seriousness of their acts and offer a way for them to change their behavior, ultimately leading to more accountable and disciplined behavior. However, should the behavior continue, further progressive measures may be warranted such as demotion, suspension and even termination.

Discipline for Growth

When appropriately used, discipline can promote both personal and professional development. Establishing explicit guidelines and expectations encourages responsibility and accountability among team members. Influential leaders know the field is about rerouting behavior into a more advantageous and congruent course rather than exacting punishment.

Consider a situation where a team member, despite their committed efforts, is struggling to meet deadlines. A manager who comprehends the nuances of discipline would sit down with the team members to discuss any difficulties they may be encountering rather than resorting solely to reprimand. They would jointly develop time management and productivity improvement techniques, ensuring the team member's development is aided rather than constrained. This strategy encourages discipline that supports personal growth and learning.

Establishing a Culture of Accountability

Teams that are led by individuals who have the ability to enforce discipline in an appropriate manner create a culture of accountability. Such a culture encourages individuals to take responsibility for their actions, learn from their mistakes, and work together to achieve common goals. It promotes an environment where everyone recognizes and comprehends the significance of adhering to values and principles.

Resisting Retaliation: An Essential Leadership Principle

Effective leadership is contingent on resistance to retaliation in any form. Retaliation is a serious breach of ethical leadership and damages trust within a group or organization because it is frequently motivated by personal grievances, resentments, or unregulated emotions. Let's examine an instance of a leader who personified the antithesis of this idea to understand the significance of reprisal resistance fully.

Consider the inept manager from the chapter on integrity. Dave was also known for being quick to anger and had a habit of holding grudges. When Lorelle, a team member, didn't catch an accidental error on a critical assignment, Dave took a retaliatory stance during a team meeting. Instead of meeting with her in person, Dave called attention to the misstep and cast doubt on her ability in front of her peers and subordinates.

Dave's actions were motivated by personal inadequacies and an objective to embarrass Lorelle, not by a sincere desire to correct the error or create a learning opportunity for her personal growth. This instance of retaliation had several damaging consequences:

- ❖ **Trust Destroyed:** Lorelle and the rest of the crew felt misled and embarrassed. They lost faith in Dave's ability to lead because they no longer thought he had their best interests in mind.
- ❖ **Reduced Morale:** Dave's actions caused the team's morale to fall. Team members reported feeling worried, disheartened, and less inspired to work hard.
- ❖ **Reduced Collaboration:** The incident made working together harder for the team. Due to their risk of reprisals,

team members were less inclined to communicate their ideas, voice their concerns, or collaborate successfully.

❖ **High Turnover:** Over time, several team members quit the company due to the toxic workplace that Dave's vindictive leadership style created. As a result, talent was lost, and the recruitment and retention cost increased.

❖ **Negative Reputation:** Because of Dave's reputation as a vengeful leader, colleagues and superiors began to doubt his aptitude for leadership positions. Additionally, any team member from within his department was now branded as "damaged goods," affecting their growth and promotion chances.

The Power of Ethical Authority

Influential leaders put fairness, empathy, and constructive criticism before retaliation, starkly contrasting Dave's actions. They know that errors are not justifications for humiliation or punishment but rather occasions for learning and development. An effective leader discusses the problem with the team member who made the mistake, providing support and advice to encourage progress.

Furthermore, great leaders aggressively promote an environment that values open communication, trust, and a sense of safety for team members to express their ideas and concerns without worrying about consequences. Avoiding reprisals is both a moral need and a key component of good leadership. It encourages cooperation, trust, and a positive workplace atmosphere that enables people to grow professionally, learn from their mistakes, and contribute significantly. Leaders can develop an environment where people and the organization can thrive by rejecting retaliation and adopting a more favorable strategy.

Balancing Support & Discipline

In conclusion, mastering the "carrot" and "stick" dichotomy of discipline requires striking a balance between them. It requires knowing when to offer assistance, support, and constructive criticism and when to enforce fair and appropriate discipline. This strategy helps people modify their behaviors while advancing the organization's expansion and overall success. Influential leaders understand that power, when used wisely and empathetically, can help create a culture of accountability and constant growth.

Discovering Your Leadership Identity: Embracing the Act of "Faking It"

Defining your identity as a leader is crucial, regardless of whether you're a first-time manager or a CEO. So often, leaders enter their positions with high expectations set by themselves and others. Unfortunately, these expectations might not always align with their current skill set, forcing them to make a difficult decision: embrace the act of "faking it" or embrace the possibility of failure.

Choosing the "fake it 'til you make it" route may appear to be a more difficult road, but it is still transformative. Faking it is not about being dishonest; it is about deliberately exhibiting the characteristics and abilities expected of a great leader, even if one does not naturally possess them. As this behavior is repeated, it ingrains these leadership qualities in the person and shapes their brand, persona, and ultimate legacy.

The Growth of Authenticity: Building a Unique Legacy

As leaders continue to "fake it 'til they make it," they begin to see a significant transformation in their leadership personality. Although the actions and characteristics may initially seem manufactured, these traits eventually become part of their natural demeanor and style. This internal change is motivated by a genuine desire to advance, inspire, and lead successfully. Those who deliberately choose this road frequently find themselves pleasantly surprised by the capacity to change and adapt during that formidable period and throughout their careers.

Upon mastery of these skills, leaders have the chance to leave a remarkable legacy when they take the transformative road of becoming the leader they desire to be rather than the leader they initially set out to become. This legacy results from a culmination of their own experiences, decisions, and development rather than a simple replication of others. This is a testament to their dedication to greatness and steadfast pursuit of becoming the leaders their teams and companies deserve.

Tips & Tricks (Because Authority is an all-encompassing attribute, numerous actions listed below also have dedicated chapters with the aim of providing a well-defined roadmap for their execution.)

1. **Action: Embrace the Role of a Great Leader**
   - **Technique:** Start your new leadership path by adopting a great leader's persona, even if it initially seems strange. Actively seek out and embrace the characteristics, actions, and traits of exceptional leaders you admire. This includes their communication and decision-making skills, along with their ability to empathize and adapt. Immerse yourself into the role, acting it out as if you were playing a character in a movie.
   - **Benefits:** You can quickly acquire and integrate effective leadership traits by adopting the "fake it 'til you make it" philosophy and assuming the role of a great leader. These qualities eventually become second nature through

repetition, resulting in genuine leadership development and transformation. This deliberate effort to exhibit leadership excellence not only motivates people around you but also aids in creating a distinctive legacy based on your dedication to both personal and professional development. It also enables you to break any poor habits or undesirable leadership behaviors you may have previously displayed, resulting in a more comprehensive and successful leadership style.

2. **Action: Ensure Clear Communication**
   - **Technique:** Maintain clear and succinct articulation of objectives, goals, and strategies using plain language while stressing active listening and respecting team members' concerns and questions to guarantee successful communication. Foster an open environment in which people may freely express themselves. Assist them in understanding their obligations, which will improve their feeling of purpose and reduce misunderstandings and blunders.
   - **Benefit:** By encouraging a transparent and well-informed workplace, team morale will be heightened, and mistakes caused by misunderstandings will lessen. When team members know their responsibilities and the broader objectives, they are more likely to feel motivated and confident.

3. **Action: Lead by Example**
   - **Technique:** Leading by example entails demonstrating the work habits, behaviors, and values you expect of your team. It involves being punctual, conducting oneself with professionalism, and consistently upholding moral standards.
   - **Benefit:** When you regularly act how you want others to work, you establish a culture of trust and responsibility.

Team members are more likely to follow your example, creating a unified and effective team.

4. **Action: Empower & Delegate**
   - **Technique:** Delegating and empowering team members entails giving them authority as well as responsibility for decisions within their areas of expertise. The goal is to give people the freedom to accept responsibility for their work, and giving them authority will ensure their success.
   - **Benefit:** This method encourages team members' development and self-assurance while decreasing your workload. They may, in turn, demonstrate their abilities, which increases job satisfaction and advances personal development.

5. **Action: Encourage Healthy Disagreement**
   - **Technique:** Encourage team members to express alternative viewpoints and participate in productive dialogues. Create a comfortable environment for questioning assumptions and examining alternatives.
   - **Benefit:** Constructive debate prevents groupthink and leads to well-informed decisions. It demonstrates that you value critical thinking over opposing perspectives and that they have no bearing on your authority. It also encourages continuous learning and intellectual curiosity.

6. **Action: Lead Cross-Functional Teams**
   - **Technique:** Lead cross-functional teams by directing projects that require a wide range of expertise, effectively collaborating among team members with diverse backgrounds and skills, harmonizing differing perspectives and approaches, ensuring alignment with unified goals, nurturing open and transparent communication, leveraging each team member's unique skills and insights, and

promoting a holistic problem-solving approach to complex challenges.

- **Benefit:** Managing cross-functional teams demonstrates your ability to exert control over various people and situations, thereby increasing your authority. It reflects your adaptability and strengthens your leadership abilities. Furthermore, it encourages the team to solve problems holistically.

7. **Action: Be Decisive & Explain Your Rationale**
   - **Technique:** Make well-informed decisions based on available facts as soon as possible, ensuring that your decision-making process is both efficient and transparent. Even if unanimous agreement on the conclusion cannot be achieved, articulate your reasoning by explaining the different aspects you've considered.
   - **Benefit:** Your capacity to make timely and open decisions strengthens your authority. Team members are more likely to accept your judgment after learning about your thought process, even if they don't always agree with you. It ensures a sense of clarity and direction amongst the team.

8. **Action: Continuously Seek Feedback on Your Leadership**
   - **Technique:** Ask your team members and peers on a frequent basis for feedback on your leadership style, competencies, and potential areas for growth. Use this input to improve your leadership style.
   - **Benefit:** Requesting feedback demonstrates humility and a commitment to progress. Showing that you are open to growth and learning improves your authority. Your leadership develops as you change to meet your team's changing needs and expectations.

9. **Action: Advocate for Work-Life Balance**
    *   **Technique:** Promote work-life balance efforts inside your company, aggressively supporting the significance of keeping normal working hours and emphasizing employee well-being. Develop a company culture that places a high value on the seamless integration of professional and personal duties.
    *   **Benefit:** Supporting work-life balance demonstrates that you are concerned about the well-being of your employees. It shows a caring and responsible leadership style. When team members see you putting their needs first, they are more likely to respect your authority. If you apply these uncommon leadership tactics, you can project authority as a great leader in a way that promotes trust, inclusivity, and continuous advancement within your team and company.

10. **Action: Resolve Conflicts Effectively**
    *   **Technique:** Effective conflict resolution requires dealing with disputes or conflicts objectively and positively. It entails carefully listening, identifying underlying concerns, and generating beneficial solutions for all parties.
    *   **Benefit:** Effective conflict resolution encourages open communication, keeps the workplace pleasant, and prevents problems from developing. Encouragement of fairness and respect among team members enhances overall teamwork.

11. **Action: Recognize & Provide Feedback**
    *   **Technique:** Providing recognition and constructive feedback requires acknowledging and applauding your team members' efforts and accomplishments. With the use of constructive criticism, they are better able to discover their areas of strength and progress.
    *   **Benefit:** Regular praise and criticism encourage team members, raising their enthusiasm and engagement. They are

more inclined to strive for excellence and perform better when respected.

12. Action: Establish Accountability

- **Technique:** Establishing accountability requires establishing clear performance standards and holding team members responsible for their actions and outcomes. Addressing issues that develop when expectations are not fulfilled is an important aspect of preserving accountability and fostering progress, establishing an accountability culture in which team members take ownership of their work and collaborate effectively to achieve their goals.

- **Benefit:** Results are predictable and consistent with a structured environment based on accountability. Team members are likelier to assume responsibility for their tasks and meet or exceed expectations, increasing team performance and trust.

Chapter Summary

This chapter delves deeply into the fundamental characteristics that define great leadership and provides helpful tips for nurturing the essence of a true leader. To pave the path to success, leaders need to explore the intersection of personal and professional power, understand the value of emotional intelligence, and master the art of discipline. Additionally, the chapter emphasizes the significance of rejecting revenge, striving for ethical authority, and identifying one's unique leadership identity. This chapter equips leaders with innovative leadership approaches and practical methods to establish authority that generates trust, inclusivity, and a culture of constant growth within their teams and organizations. It provides a comprehensive guide for individuals striving to leave a lasting legacy as influential and effective leaders, with advice on embracing the role of a great leader, ensuring clear communication, leading by example, and much more.

CHAPTER 3

THE POWER OF GRIT:
THE VALUE OF HARD WORK & HUMILITY

The most commendable attribute is humility, mixed with a strong work ethic. In the pursuit of leadership greatness, this chapter examines the crucial value of working hard, doing more than one's share, letting go of entitlement, and resisting the allure of martyrdom.

Hard Work: The Source of Achievement

A strong work ethic is the foundation upon which great leadership is based. Rolling up their sleeves, getting involved in the day-to-day problems, and leading by example convey a powerful message that success is a continual journey marked by unshakable devotion and loyalty.

Consider Elon Musk's amazing journey as the visionary driving SpaceX, Tesla, and a plethora of ground-breaking ventures, including PayPal, The Boring Company, and xAI. Musk's relentless work ethic has served as a driving force in all of his ventures. His dedication to accomplishing his lofty ambitions knows no bounds. Musk is regularly seen working long hours, sleeping in his office, and thoroughly immersing himself in his businesses. His solid commitment to innovation has left an indelible impression on a wide range of industries.

Elon Musk's extraordinary work ethic and tenacity have propelled him to success in companies like SpaceX, Tesla, The Boring Company, and xAI. With SpaceX, he is pushing the boundaries of space technology in order to reach interplanetary colonization. He has transformed the electric vehicle industry and revolutionized the entire approach to automotive manufacturing and sales. His commitment extends to The Boring Company, where he seeks to transform transportation infrastructure by utilizing subterranean tunnel networks. xAI is the company's research and development unit for cutting-edge artificial intelligence solutions. Musk's tale is an example of the transforming power of tenacity and visionary leadership.

Leaders like Elon Musk, who exemplify endurance, inspire their teams to strive for greatness. When team members see their leader's persistent devotion, they are motivated to put their sweat and effort into the common goal. A strong work ethic spreads like wildfire, advancing a culture of continuous achievement.

In today's society, when someone's worth is measured by how much they contribute to their workplace, as well as what they provide for their family and community, the significance of productivity and a strong work ethic cannot be stressed enough. These characteristics are not only highly regarded, but they frequently serve as the cornerstone for professional and personal success.

Unwavering Consistency in Delivering Results

Great leadership is defined by its consistent delivery of results that teams admire, and businesses rely on. It is not only about achieving success once but about achieving it consistently across numerous hurdles and ever-changing terrain. Exceptional leaders set the bar high by regularly producing measurable results, whether it's reaching targets, encouraging innovation, or consistently offering value. Their dependability and consistency instill trust and confidence in their people, pushing them to strive for greater heights and driving the company's long-term success.

Harmonizing with Organizational Objectives

Building people and environments that function in harmony with corporate goals is associated with great leadership. It's not only about creating a vision; it's about encouraging people to match their efforts, abilities, and passion with the organization's larger goals. Exceptional leaders see the value of building a cohesive team in which each member's abilities complement one another, and a shared sense of purpose motivates growth. They foster an environment in which every team member feels respected and empowered, where open communication is encouraged, and where individuals are encouraged to offer their best efforts to achieve common goals. Great leadership pulls together a team's different abilities and energies, creating a dynamic synergy that propels the organization toward its goals.

Humble & Driven Attitude

To thrive in a competitive business environment, you must have a modest yet determined mentality. Individuals with a sense of humility stay open to learning and are responsive to criticism, allowing continuous improvement. A motivated mindset is more likely to remain focused, persistent, and willing to put in the effort required for success.

In parallel with Sun Tzu's "The Art of War," one may infer that humility may pave the way for self-understanding, awareness of strengths and weaknesses, and the avoidance of underestimating opponents—an indispensable trait, even in corporate environments. Despite misunderstandings, these attributes aren't weaknesses but formidable strengths. Embracing humility fuels ongoing learning, while openness ignites collaboration—both pivotal for success in strategic warfare and navigating the competitive intricacies of the corporate world.

Paying Your Dues: The Path to Mastery

Being a leader is a process, not an entitlement. Paying one's dues is essential because it teaches one that mastery requires time, effort, and a willingness to learn from both successes and mistakes. They admit that every experience, no matter how insignificant, helps them grow as leaders.

Satya Nadella's path to becoming Microsoft's CEO illustrates his constant commitment to learning and personal development. Nadella began his career at Microsoft as a junior engineer. He painstakingly climbed the corporate ladder from these low beginnings, collecting vital expertise at each step. This voyage taught him the value of hands-on experience and the constant improvement of his talents.

Nadella's rise inside the firm was about more than just securing promotions; it was also about mastering his craft. He gained a profound understanding of Microsoft's inner workings, culture, and the computer sector as a whole as he took on increasingly difficult roles. This hands-on experience was crucial in defining his leadership style and strategic ideas, which he would eventually apply to the post of CEO.

His rise was not meteoric but was marked by a persistent dedication to personal development and a continuous quest for excellence. This strategy meant that when the opportunity to manage the company arose, he was well-prepared and armed with the experience, talents, and insights that would eventually shape him into the transformational leader he is today. Nadella's journey highlights the crucial role of amassing experience and paying one's dues in acquiring the capabilities and insights required for effective leadership at the highest levels.

Shunning Entitlement: The Antithesis of Leadership

Great leadership is opposed to entitlement. Leaders who feel exempt from hard effort or believe they are owed success without trying risk alienating and eroding their employees' trust. Entitlement obscures the need for self-improvement and the necessity to support a shared cause.

Earned leadership, on the other hand, is distinguished by humility. Humble leaders recognize that they are members of a team and that no one is perfect. They request input from their teams, are conscious of their limits, and are open to different points of view.

Warren Buffett, widely regarded as one of history's most successful investors and a great model of leadership humility, is notable for his exceptional, down-to-earth manner. Buffett's feet remain firmly on the ground despite his enormous riches and track record of exceptional accomplishments. He leads a simple existence, embracing a humble way of living that is distant from the luxury commonly associated with vast wealth.

What distinguishes Buffett's leadership style is his insistence on being grounded and avoiding any sense of entitlement. He recognizes that humility is not only a personal virtue but also a necessary attribute in leadership. He understands that his accomplishments are the result of hard work, excellent judgment, and a bit of luck, and he continually communicates this understanding to his colleagues and those who look up to him.

Buffett's affable and friendly personality reflects his humble nature, making him easily relatable to individuals from all walks of life. His capacity to connect with others on a human level, as well as his openness to learn from anybody, regardless of background or status, distinguishes him as a leader. Warren Buffett is a timeless illustration of how humility can be a vital attribute in leadership in a culture marked by ostentation and ego. His legacy emphasizes the value of keeping modest, grounded, and committed to lifelong learning, inspiring those around him to do the same, and supporting the notion that entitlement has no place in good leadership.

Martyrdom: The Pitfall of Excessive Sacrifice

Being viewed as a martyr is not required for leadership. Even when long hours and hard effort are necessary, leaders must strike a balance between devotion and self-care. Overcommitment can lead to burnout and hinder one's ability to lead effectively. Leaders can set an example by prioritizing self-care and maintaining work-life balance, recognizing that leadership is a marathon, not a sprint.

Tips & Tricks

1. **Action: Commit to Daily Improvement**
   - **Technique:** As part of your commitment to continual development, set aside time daily to enhance your talents, knowledge, or work practices. Prioritize little, everyday steps toward progress, such as reading relevant articles, acquiring new skills, or honing your problem-solving abilities. Regarding leadership training, utilize this reference guidebook as an outline to continue learning about each trait and characteristic through further research via books, video lectures, internet articles, etc.
   - **Benefits:** Committing to everyday development helps you build a growth mindset and inspires others to do the same. It leads to continual skill growth, increased adaptability, and a learning culture within the team.

2. **Action: Embrace Challenges**
   - **Technique:** Look for complicated activities or projects, especially if they are outside the scope of your responsibilities and/or comfort zone.
   - **Benefits:** Accepting problems as a leader demonstrates resiliency and bravery. It pushes your staff to face difficult situations head-on and motivates them to be bold and

creative. You will find the road to exceptional achievements is paved with difficulties.

3. **Action: Stay Adaptable**
   - **Technique:** Maintain your adaptability by assessing your management style and working methods on a regular basis. Be open to criticism and ready to adjust your approach if necessary. A flexible leadership style sets a great example for your team.
   - **Benefits:** By being adaptable, the team promotes an agile and innovative culture. It motivates individuals to embrace change and seek out more efficient ways of doing business. Furthermore, it allows your team to respond quickly to new challenges and opportunities. Teams that get stuck in their ways become obsolete.

4. **Action: Demonstrate Perseverance**
   - **Technique:** Demonstrate persistence in the face of setbacks and failures. Even when things are challenging, keep going and have an upbeat mindset. Demonstrate that with work and determination, challenges can be overcome.
   - **Benefits:** When you exhibit perseverance, your team will become more resilient. It motivates team members to continue in the face of adversity and creates a "never give up" attitude.

5. **Action: Set the Example**
   - **Technique:** Setting the example includes consistently demonstrating a high work ethic via actions such as early arrival, staying late when necessary, and taking on challenging projects. It also includes exhibiting dedication to the team's goals and going above and beyond to achieve them. Your commitment to your work sets the standard for the quality of work produced by your team.

- **Benefits:** When you lead by example, your team members will see a clear example of what a hard day's work looks like. Because people are more likely to appreciate and admire your dedication, it may motivate them to work more. This nurtures a culture of grit and determination in which everyone strives for success.

6. **Action: Efficient Time Management**
   - **Technique:** Setting priorities, defining goals, and utilizing productivity tools are all components of efficient time management. To maximize efficiency during working hours, eliminate procrastination, and minimize distractions. Your ability to manage your time effectively indicates your commitment to making the most of each day.
   - **Benefits:** Effective time management allows you to finish more duties while also demonstrating that you are disciplined and organized. Your team notices how you successfully handle several responsibilities, setting a fantastic example for them to follow.

7. **Action: Visible & Accessible**
   - **Technique:** When it comes to working with your team, it's important to be present and approachable. This includes traveling around the office, attending team meetings, and setting up one-on-one meetings. It demonstrates that you are there and ready to assist your team.
   - **Benefits:** Being visible and available to your team members is key to building strong relationships and fostering a collaborative work environment. Your presence promotes open communication and trust. Problem-solving and teamwork enhance when team members feel comfortable approaching you with questions, concerns, or recommendations. It also promotes friendship and a sense of solidarity among team members.

8. **Action: Consistent & On-Time Results**
   - **Technique:** Delivering on your commitments and meeting or exceeding performance requirements on a regular basis are all instances of achieving consistent success. It necessitates a dedication to perfection, a keen eye for detail, and a strong work ethic.
   - **Benefits:** Your trustworthy track record instills confidence in your abilities. Team members feel comfortable and stable working with you since they know they can rely on you to accomplish the task. It also demonstrates that hard work pays rewards, motivating others to strive for their best.

9. **Action: Transparent Communication & Humble Progress Promotion**
   - **Technique:** Transparent communication requires being open and honest while communicating your efforts, challenges, and victories with your team. It entails providing regular project updates, admitting mistakes, and cooperating to find solutions. When highlighting your successes, be humble and focus on the team rather than just individual efforts.
   - **Benefits:** Transparent communication promotes team humility while displaying ownership and commitment to finding solutions. It motivates your employees to follow suit, promoting a culture of collaboration, humility, and accountability. This method encourages team transparency and trust, which boosts morale and productivity. It also guarantees that everyone receives appreciation, creating team cohesiveness.

10. **Action: Embrace Humble Language**
    - **Technique:** When conveying their accomplishments and efforts, great leaders display humility and collaboration by using "we" or "team" instead of "I." This strategy

emphasizes the organization's joint efforts and shared achievement. Leaders offer gratitude to the team and stress the collaborative work that contributed to their accomplishments when recognizing successes. They consciously avoid self-centered rhetoric and acknowledge that it is the team's collective abilities and passion that drive outcomes.

- **Benefit:** Humble language promotes a culture of collaboration and teamwork. It instills in team members a sense of belonging and shared ownership. Leaders raise morale and motivation by attributing achievement to the team's joint efforts. This method promotes trust and loyalty among team members by making them feel appreciated and acknowledged for their work. In the long run, using modest language builds stronger, more cohesive teams and leads to long-term organizational success.

Chapter Summary

Excellent leadership is built on a dedication to hard work and genuine humility. In this chapter, we explore the importance of endurance, paying one's dues, relinquishing entitlement, and avoiding martyrdom on the path to leadership greatness. Leaders who uphold these principles inspire their teams, promote a goal-oriented culture, and drive success. These characteristics help individuals advance in their careers and contribute to the success of their organizations. Great leaders are assessed not just on how successfully they accomplish their jobs in this fast-paced, fiercely competitive corporate world but also on how they impact their families and communities within their personal lives.

CHAPTER 4

COMMUNICATION:
THE MAKE-OR-BREAK SKILL

Excellent communication skills are the cornerstone of success. The ability of a competent and outstanding leader to effectively communicate thoughts, ideas, and vision may differ. In this chapter, we'll look at the important effects of efficient communication in leadership, such as how it may boost influence and team cohesiveness.

Clarity: Clear Vision, Clear Decisions

Clear and succinct communication is the foundation of well-informed decision-making. Effective communicators can explain the reasoning behind their decisions, reducing the likelihood of misunderstandings or blunders. In a world where decisions may have far-reaching consequences, effective communication is the compass that keeps leaders and their teams aligned on their path to success.

Trust Building: The Foundation of Success

Trust is the foundation of every successful team or organization, and it flourishes in an environment of open and honest communication. Team members are more inclined to trust leaders who communicate openly, acknowledging both triumphs and troubles. When people trust each other, they are more willing to collaborate, take risks, and perform their best in their jobs.

Employee Engagement: Fueling the Fire of Motivation

If trust is the engine, communication is the fuel for a motivated and engaged team. Influential executives keep their staff informed, engaged, and invested in the success of the organization. Employees who are involved are more likely to go above and beyond, support innovation, and provide exceptional outcomes.

Crisis Management: Leading Through Chaos

The need for effective communication becomes especially clear at times of struggle or disaster. Leaders who communicate with their teams in a calm, assured, and compassionate manner provide guidance and assurance. Their remarks serve as a sense of stability in the midst of chaos.

Great leaders have an extraordinary ability not only to communicate but also to move the depths of the human spirit. They have the ability to inspire folks to achieve amazing feats by uniting them under a shared mission through the creative use of words and the power of their delivery. Consider Winston Churchill's wartime speeches during World War II, when his words acted as a beacon of hope and determination for nations facing tragedy. In the face of extraordinary obstacles, his eloquence and unflinching resolve roused the national spirit and inspired a revitalized sense of purpose.

Similarly, consider the transforming influence of Martin Luther King Jr.'s civil rights lectures, which were not simple words but blazing sparks that ignited the American civil rights movement. King's speeches were a rallying cry for justice, equality, and togetherness, motivating people from all walks of life to come together in the face of injustice. His comments were a catalyst for change, demonstrating the incredible power of excellent communication to move hearts, alter minds, and shape history.

The Efficacy Great Communication Skills

Ronald Reagan, dubbed the "Great Communicator," provides a striking example of how effective communication can influence successful leadership. His motivational speeches, such as the famous "Tear Down This Wall" address in Berlin, not only captured the hearts and minds of millions but were also critical to Germany's final unification. Reagan's remarkable effect was demonstrated by his ability to convey a clear vision of a unified world.

Reagan's economic initiatives, named "Reaganomics," demonstrate his ability to see the big picture. Through his persuasive and direct speech, he articulated his view of reducing government involvement in the economy and championed free-market ideals. Because of this concept, the United States had a period of fast economic expansion.

Reagan's crisis-management abilities during the Cold War and in the aftermath of the Challenger disaster emphasized the significance of clear communication in difficult situations. He brought stability and optimism to the country by demonstrating assurance, calmness, and persistence in the face of adversity.

Ronald Reagan illustrated how excellent communication skills can enhance one's ability to influence, provide clarity of goal, and elegantly resolve obstacles. His legacy demonstrates the long-term importance of excellent communication in leadership.

Tips & Tricks

1. **Action: Transparency & Authenticity**
   - **Technique:** Authentic communication is openly addressing your goals, expectations, and obstacles, as well as sharing pertinent updates with your team on a regular basis. Encourage team members' ideas and feedback while establishing a culture of openness via open and honest communication. Create open discussion venues, such as team

meetings or feedback sessions, to participate in two-way communication that values honesty and sincerity.

- **Benefit:** Transparency and authenticity generate trust and credibility, which improves relationships and advances an open and stimulating work environment. Furthermore, honest and open communication encourages others to do the same.

2. **Action: Pacing for Impact**

- **Technique:** Be aware of the flow of your conversation. Adapt the tempo of your speech to the preferences of the audience and the complexity of the content. Slowing down and allowing for pauses can sometimes improve learning and retention.

- **Benefit:** By carefully selecting your speed, you may prevent information overload and transmit your message at an understandable rate. It also makes it easier for your audience to absorb and comprehend information.

3. **Action: Silence as a Communication Tool**

- **Technique:** Recognize the importance of silence in communicating. Allowing moments of silence to pass can frequently be more useful than speaking throughout every pause.

- **Benefit:** Silent communication encourages thorough thought, relieves strain on the speaker, and encourages a more forgiving and caring atmosphere. It gives individuals undisturbed time to process information, formulate replies, and express their ideas. It also allows for greater in-depth comprehension and replies in communication.

4. **Action: The "What Else?" Question**
   - **Technique:** Encourage active participation in discussions by urging team members to offer more by asking them, "What else is going on?" or simply, "What else?" Encourage them to provide any new thoughts, opinions, or important information that was not initially addressed.
   - **Benefit:** Placing the "what else" inquiry in context stimulates in-depth thinking, the discovery of hidden concepts, and the cultivation of a full comprehension of the subject. It also elicits information about other activities, ideas, or questions, which enhances the dialogue. Because they know you'll be checking in on their work on a regular basis, it sets the expectation for your team to sustain high output levels. These components work together to improve overall team decision-making and communication abilities.

5. **Action: Becoming a Captivating Speaker**
   - **Technique:** To hone your communication style as a great leader, immerse yourself in the study of speeches made by excellent orators. View a range of talks, including historical leaders, TED Talks, significant movie sequences, and even televangelists. Pay attention to not only the words spoken but also to the rhythm, vocal tone, facial gestures, body language, and emotional effect. Take notes on the approaches that appeal to you and examine how they evoke emotion and motivation in their audience.
   - **Benefit:** By studying the tactics of great orators, you may improve your ability to inspire, encourage, and connect with your team. Learning to harness the power of effective communication will enhance your leadership by helping you to communicate your message with greater impact and authenticity, building a stronger emotional connection with the people you lead.

6. **Action: Multimodal Communication**
   - **Technique:** Accept a multimodal communication strategy. To explain complicated topics, use images, graphs, charts, multimedia presentations, and interactive verbal and written communication. Combine these various mediums to create dynamic and engaging presentations.
   - **Benefit:** Multimodal communication allows for greater audience reach, as well as improved comprehension and retention of information, especially when interactive aspects are employed. Varying the pace through the use of different methods also captures and maintains the audience's interest, contributing to enhanced engagement.

7. **Action: Create "Sound Bites"**
   - **Technique:** Create "Sound Bites," which are small, relevant communication "nuggets" that simplify complex concepts or messages. You can enhance the memorability of your message by connecting it to something your team already understands.
   - **Benefit:** Sound bites can help your team learn and remember difficult topics. They boost your authority by demonstrating your ability to distill difficult ideas into simple insights, which encourages better comprehension and retention. It also decreases the possibility of the message being misconstrued later on.

8. **Action: Implement Comprehensive Written Recaps**
   - **Technique:** A strong leader ensures efficient communication by establishing detailed written recaps of meetings, negotiations, performance reviews, disciplinary actions, and policy changes. Following any critical encounter or decision-making process, the leader should take the initiative to write down essential points, agreements, or changes discussed. To provide clarity and serve as a

reference for all parties involved, this review should include details such as action items, timelines, and responsibilities.

- **Benefit:** Implementing complete written recaps is an important communication tactic for a successful leader. By summarizing critical information in writing, the leader reduces the likelihood of misunderstandings, ensures team member alignment, and offers a clear record of choices and expectations. This method improves organizational openness, accountability, and overall communication efficacy, resulting in smoother operations and building a culture of clarity and shared understanding.

9. **Action: Cultivate Digital Communication Etiquette**
   - **Technique:** In the digital era, online chats may still be useful means of communication. Develop acceptable digital communication skills, such as timely email answers, courteous and professional written communication, and an understanding of digital privacy and security. Any correspondence over three lengthy emails deserves a person-to-person discussion, whether it is via phone or, better yet, in person.
   - **Benefit:** Sound digital communication practices build professionalism, trust, and successful online connections. They reduce the likelihood of misunderstandings or poor communication in virtual environments. The idea of person-to-person discussion recognizes the limitations of written communication and highlights the value of direct, real-time interaction for more complex or crucial matters.

10. **Action: Bridge Cultural Communication Gaps**
    - **Technique:** In multicultural settings, be proactive in overcoming cultural communication barriers. Learn about cultural norms, conventions, and sensitivities that may influence how messages are perceived. Your communication

style should be adjusted to accommodate different cultural perspectives.

- **Benefit:** The benefits of doing so include increased cross-cultural dialogue and a lesser probability of miscommunication or accidental offending. It promotes inclusion and appreciation for diversity within your team or organization.

11. Action: Nonverbal Communication

- **Technique:** Nonverbal cues such as body language, facial expressions, and tone of voice have a significant impact on communication. Make sure your nonverbal cues support the message you want to convey. Maintain an open body language and adjust your tone to come across as sincere and empathic.
- **Benefit:** Effective nonverbal communication increases the reliability of your message, reduces misinterpretations, and reinforces your desired tone.

12. Action: Visual Listening

- **Technique:** Develop visual listening skills by paying attention to people's facial expressions, body language, and general mood while actively processing their communication content. Subtle indications, such as changes in posture, gestures, or eye contact, should be noted and linked to the message being given. Empathetic observation and genuine attention can be demonstrated by appropriate nonverbal reactions such as nodding, keeping eye contact, or imitating pleasant gestures.
- **Benefit:** Visual cues may frequently communicate sentiments and thoughts that words cannot. Visual listening enhances your ability to comprehend others more thoroughly. It enables you to recognize nonverbal cues and respond to their needs and concerns in a more efficient and

empathetic manner. This strategy promotes better communication and aids in conflict resolution.

13. **Action: "Being in the Moment"**
   - **Technique:** Effective communicators excel at active listening. By "Being in the Moment" and giving your complete attention while maintaining eye contact and avoiding distractions, you show respect for the speaker, ensuring you thoroughly absorb the message before answering.
   - **Benefit:** Active listening enhances comprehension, reduces misunderstandings, and develops interpersonal bonds by making others feel heard and appreciated.

14. **Action: Empathetic Communication**
   - **Technique:** Empathy is a necessary component of effective communication. Make an attempt to understand and empathize with the emotions and perspectives of others. Validate people's experiences and emotions to build trust and connections.
   - **Benefit:** Empathic communication creates a more collaborative and supportive atmosphere while also promoting trust, empathy, and stronger interpersonal connections.

15. **Action: Kid Speak: Adapting Your Message**
   - **Technique:** Apply this concept to your interpersonal connections, much as you would change your tone of voice when interacting with children vs. adults. Recognize that different methods of communication are preferred by other people, and adjust your speaking habits accordingly. Change the formality, degree of information, or depth of your message to match the situation and the people involved.

- **Benefit:** When you embrace diversity in your communication strategies, you increase your ability to communicate successfully with a variety of audiences in a variety of circumstances. This flexibility significantly increases effective communication by accommodating the preferences of listeners, no matter how particular they are.

16. **Action: The Storyteller's Edge**
    - **Technique:** Storytelling is a powerful mode of communication. To demonstrate your points and emotionally connect with your audience, use relatable stories, anecdotes, or tales.
    - **Benefit:** Stories assist your audience in grasping and recalling difficult concepts, allowing you to build a closer bond with them. Storytelling improves the efficacy and persuasiveness of communication by increasing audience connection, emotional involvement, and message retention.

Chapter Summary

By sparking and motivating the team behind a common purpose, effective communication first increases a leader's impact. Second, it encourages improved decision-making by increasing clarity and reducing misconceptions. Third, a culture that emphasizes open and honest communication develops trust, which is one of the fundamental components of effective teams. Fourth, leaders with effective communication skills manage difficulties in a way that promotes productive debate and solutions. Finally, good communication is key for building employee enthusiasm and devotion, as well as innovation and exceptional results. This chapter also discusses useful communication techniques such as active listening, clarity, empathy, nonverbal signs, adaptability, feedback solicitation, and the persuasiveness of storytelling.

CHAPTER 5

DECISIVE LEADERSHIP:
MAKING BOLD CHOICES WITH CONFIDENCE

Decisiveness is the foundation of effective decision-making, empowering leaders in every industry to boldly confront the challenges of their roles with confidence.

Timely Decision-Making

Decisiveness is a leadership trait that recognizes hesitation as a formidable opponent. Strong leaders understand the importance of timely decisions in the advancement of enterprises. Decisive leaders avoid the pitfalls of "analysis paralysis," characterized by an overwhelming volume of information causing indecision and inaction. Instead, they carefully evaluate the available facts, assess potential risks, and take prompt action.

Consider a scenario in the technology business in which a CEO must make a critical decision about the introduction of a new product. A decisive CEO solicits feedback from their employees, assesses the situation of the market, and makes an educated choice promptly. Their ability to make quick decisions puts them ahead of competitors and creates trust in their employees.

Decisive leaders keep their teams from becoming mired in uncertainty. Their influence is strengthened by their ability to make judgments that keep the ship on course even in rough seas.

The Embrace of Clarity & Focus

Decisiveness is a driving force that reveals the path ahead. Excellent leaders instill confidence and clarity in their teams, ensuring that everyone fully understands the goals and direction with pinpoint accuracy.

Let us look back in time and consider Winston Churchill's exceptional leadership throughout World War II. Churchill's decisiveness was not merely a question of choice as he sailed the perilous seas of war but an imperative necessity. In a difficult period, his unflinching determination to confront tyranny and lead the United Kingdom to victory provided much-needed clarity.

Churchill's determined actions during the war served as a tactical battle strategy. His orders and remarks struck a connection with the masses, inspiring fearless dedication to the cause. His ability to speak plainly and without ambiguity galvanized his compatriots to give it their best, resulting in triumph.

Winston Churchill epitomizes the power of decisiveness in leadership. His resolute commitment to clarity and focus bolstered his authority, illustrating how decisive leadership may be the key to success in tremendous adversity by illuminating the path forward with steadfast conviction.

The Commitment to Efficient Action

In the fast-paced world of leadership, decisiveness is not synonymous with haste. It entails making successful judgments that promote the organization's goals. Decisive leaders recognize the need to pay meticulous attention to detail in carrying out their decisions.

Consider a plant CEO entrusted with enhancing the manufacturing process. A decisive CEO ensures that reforms are implemented successfully, as well as identifying opportunities for development. The benefits of this commitment to efficiency include cost savings, increased output, and a competitive advantage in the market.

Leaders who make decisions thoroughly evaluate the implications of their decisions and prioritize their execution. Their authority is strengthened by their ability to create outcomes via careful and effective decision-making.

The Balance of Delegation & Responsibility

Throughout my career, I've encountered leaders who either grasp or fail to comprehend the delicate balance between delegating and responsibility. Those who understand it, such as astute hospitality managers, for example, empower their personnel by delegating responsibility and decision-making authority while keeping ultimate control over the guest experience. Individuals who fall short, on the other hand, typically fail, resulting in disgruntled consumers, misunderstandings, and missed opportunities for advancement. Their inability to strike the optimum balance between delegation and accountability may lead to a breakdown in cooperation, a deterioration in trust, and, finally, a decrease in the organization's performance and success. It underlines the need to understand this essential component of leadership in order to navigate the complexities of the business world successfully.

Consider the role of a hotel general manager who empowers department heads to make decisions that will boost client satisfaction. This delegation, in addition to empowering team members, frees the general manager to focus on broad initiatives. However, the general manager is still in charge of ensuring that every tourist receives outstanding service.

You may encounter situations where the outcome is unknown or where you must make a decision quickly, so bear in mind that no decision-making technique is perfect. Flexibility and the capacity to learn from your decisions, whether successful or not, become equally important components of being a great decision-maker under these circumstances. With practice and reflection, you can polish your decision-making abilities and become more adept at making sound judgments in a range of situations.

Tips & Tricks

1. **Action: Leverage Information Warfare**
   - **Technique:** It's amazing how many individuals fail to do this. To begin good decision-making, it is important first to gather a large amount of relevant knowledge. Sun Tzu suggested using information warfare. In keeping with Sun Tzu's emphasis on the use of intelligence in fighting, gather and evaluate data relevant to your industry, competitors, and market trends: "Know yourself, know your opponent, and you will never be in danger in a hundred conflicts."
   - **Benefit:** Decision-makers boost their chances of making well-informed judgments that take into consideration all important factors and provide a comprehensive understanding of the situation at hand by carefully gathering information. As a consequence, judgments are more likely to be successful, and there is less danger of making mistakes or omissions, which can occur when there is inadequate information. While this approach may take longer initially, it will pay off if the original choice is incorrect and results in more costs, arduous effort, embarrassment, a loss of team spirit, or reputational injury.

2. **Action: Just Say No to Analysis Paralysis**
   - **Technique:** Recognize that the fear of making the wrong decision frequently leads to over-analyzing and procrastination... Analysis Paralysis. To avoid falling into

this trap, create a decision-making framework that includes priority criteria and a non-negotiable deadline. Keep this concept in mind throughout the process.

- **Benefit:** By breaking away from the grip of analytical paralysis and using this strategy, you empower yourself to overcome hesitations caused by a lack of confidence or a fear of making a mistake. Prioritizing criteria guarantees that you focus on the most important variables, while meeting a deadline forces you to move quickly and make a choice. This method not only encourages more efficient and effective decision-making, but it also reduces the load of unneeded busy work for you and your team, accelerates progress, and boosts morale, generating a more dynamic and confident decision-making atmosphere.

3. **Action: Establish Decision Criteria**
   - **Technique:** Establish well-defined decision criteria that are linked with your aims and objectives to ensure successful decision-making. These criteria must be explicit, quantifiable, and pertinent to the issue. For example, if you're deciding between two possible initiatives, consider aspects such as estimated return on investment, alignment with the company's objective, and resource availability.
   - **Benefits:** Establishing decision criteria simplifies the decision-making process by providing a systematic structure. It ensures that judgments are made on the basis of relevant knowledge, reducing the chance of being affected by irrelevant information or personal preconceptions.

4. **Action: Simulate Future Financial Scenarios**
   - **Technique:** Carry out scenario planning by modeling probable future implications based on various options. This method comprises keeping track of the consequences of

each choice and assessing their impact on many aspects of your company.

- **Benefits:** Simulating probable future occurrences provides decision-makers with a forward-looking perspective, which helps them make better decisions. It assists you in predicting upcoming financial challenges and possibilities, allowing you to make decisions that are consistent with your long-term strategic goals.

5. **Action: Leverage Data Visualization**
   - **Technique:** Use data visualization tools such as charts, graphs, and dashboards to improve your data-driven decision-making. Select the best data visualization method for your situation: bar charts for comparisons, line graphs for trends. Maintain simplicity and avoid complications. Maintain color-coding and labeling uniformity. Include context by providing explanations and insights. For more engagement, use interactive visualizations. Update on a regular basis to guarantee the most recent information.
   - **Benefits:** Data visualization facilitates information comprehension, enabling faster and more informed decisions. Making results visually appealing promotes clarity and supports data-driven decisions.

6. **Action: Apply Ethical Decision-Making**
   - **Technique:** Make an effort to include ethical considerations in all of your decisions. Consider how each decision aligns with your company's principles, ethics, and social responsibility.
   - **Benefits:** Making ethical judgments ensures that decisions are consistent with moral and cultural norms. It establishes an ethical culture inside the organization and helps to build trust, reputation, and moral leadership.

7. **Action: Build a Decision-Making Culture**
    - **Technique:** Allowing team members to make decisions within their areas of expertise can help to develop a decision-making culture inside your organization. Encourage and support them as they work to enhance their decision-making abilities.
    - **Benefits:** By building a decision-making culture, businesses may respond more rapidly and be more flexible by sharing decision-making responsibilities. It also motivates team members to improve their leadership abilities, resulting in a more adaptive and proactive workforce.

8. **Action: Conduct Decision Audits**
    - **Technique:** Periodically review and assess previous selections to identify lessons learned and areas for improvement. Consider the outcomes and consequences of prior decisions to enhance your decision-making process.
    - **Benefits:** Decision audits promote continuous decision-making improvement. They help to strengthen decision-making skills, reduce the likelihood of repeating errors, and increase the quality of future decisions.

9. **Action: No More Knee Jerk: Decisions Without Regret**
    - **Technique:** Before making crucial decisions, take a moment to reflect. This includes pausing to collect your thoughts, disconnect from your feelings, and focus on the present moment. Deep breathing or mindfulness methods are additional head-clearing techniques used to keep individuals from making rash decisions. Take this time to evaluate the quality and quantity of decision-making material on hand. If the amount is insufficient, take the opportunity to seek more information.

- **Benefits:** The mindful pause technique helps decision-making by reducing tension and anxiety, allowing for a more calm and thoughtful approach and minimizing the knee-jerk reaction of making an emotional decision. It promotes mental clarity, ensuring that decisions are made with a calm, collected mind.

10. Action: Beyond the Obvious

- **Technique:** Instead of leaping to a conclusion, decision-makers might study a number of potential options by assessing alternatives to what has been provided. This method promotes flexibility and uniqueness, broadening the number of options. Just because it is the first or most popular answer doesn't make it the best answer.
- **Benefit:** A wide range of possibilities stimulates innovation and creativity, which leads to sound decision-making. It enables decision-makers to look at more options and come up with more effective and sometimes groundbreaking solutions.

11. Action: Assess Risks & Benefits

- **Technique:** Making educated selections necessitates carefully considering the possible risks and benefits of each option. This approach comprises a detailed evaluation of both immediate and long-term consequences, providing a complete picture of the decision's consequences.
- **Benefit:** By assessing the risks and rewards, decision-makers have a better understanding of the consequences of their actions. This leads to more deliberate decision-making that is balanced and focused on minimizing potential drawbacks while boosting advantages.

12. **Action: Gather Additional Information**
    - **Technique:** When presented with a circumstance where various points of view impede decision-making, take proactive actions to get more information. Make certain that all parties involved have access to the essential facts, research, and insights on the choice at hand. To overcome any information gaps, encourage open communication and knowledge exchange among team members.
    - **Benefit:** Gathering more information addresses two essential facets of good decision-making. For starters, it addresses the issue of insufficient objective facts, guaranteeing that the choice is based on a thorough grasp of the circumstance. Secondly, it encourages informed team conversations, lowering the chance of viewpoints being affected by inadequate facts. This strategy promotes well-informed and consensus-driven decision-making, which leads to more successful outcomes.

13. **Action: Use Decision-Making Frameworks**
    - **Technique:** Using decision-making frameworks such as SWOT analysis, cost-benefit analysis, and decision trees can help in options appraisal. Because of these tools, the decision-making process is more ordered and objective.
    - **Benefit:** When decision-making frameworks are employed, the decision-making process becomes more structured and objective, which enhances its organization and transparency. As a result, decision-making becomes more structured and informed.

14. **Action: Seek Objective Input & Feedback**
    - **Technique:** When seeking advice and views from others, it is critical to prioritize objectivity over personal preferences. It requires gathering perspectives that contradict one's own ideas and provide a thorough grasp of the option.

- **Benefit:** Asking for impartial viewpoints and criticism leads to more well-rounded and solid conclusions. It helps decision-makers avoid needless biases based on their personal viewpoints and ensures that judgments are made based on the relative merits of the available options.

15. Action: Avoid Collateral Damage

- **Technique:** Unfortunately, there is another seemingly easy step that many people overlook. A leader must be aware of everyone who will be affected by their actions. Spend some time identifying every stakeholder—internal, external, and the plethora of others "down the line"—who may be impacted by your actions. This method should include examining potential negative consequences and making decisions while keeping your business and clients in mind.
- **Benefits:** You may reduce collateral damage and unexpected results by becoming fully aware of the ramifications of your decisions. This technique ensures that your judgments are well-informed and consider all important factors. Furthermore, it nurtures a culture of responsible and caring leadership, reduces reputational harm, and maintains strong team morale.

Chapter Summary

Leaders may utilize decisiveness to boldly and clearly negotiate the challenges of their positions across all sectors. Decisiveness is a leadership trait that recognizes hesitation as a formidable opponent. Great leaders are not influenced by analytical paralysis and acknowledge the need for timely choices that keep businesses moving forward. A decisive leader ensures that everyone on their team understands the goals and direction because they recognize that clarity and concentration are critical drivers of productivity and success. They also value paying close attention to detail in the execution of their judgments and are committed to taking efficient action, which means making decisions that are efficient and compatible with the company's objectives. Finally, decisive leaders understand how to strike the correct balance between delegation and accountability, delegating tasks and decision-making authority to their teams while remaining ultimately accountable for the results.

CHAPTER 6

LEADING WITH IMAGINATION: THE SYNERGY OF VISION AND CREATIVITY

Vision and innovation are two powerful factors propelling firms to greatness. This chapter emphasizes the crucial importance of these two pillars by demonstrating how they promote change, stimulate innovation, and drive groups to achieve bigger things.

Vision: Navigating the Uncharted Waters

Leaders are like a ship's navigators, charting uncharted territory. Their vision, a clear, compelling image of the future they want to build, acts as a guidepost. A compelling vision provides leaders and their teams with direction, purpose, and inspiration.

Martin Luther King Jr. brilliantly envisioned a future with better fairness and equity in his famous "I Have a Dream" speech. His views sparked a civil rights movement that changed the course of history and brought the country together. King's untiring commitment to his vision demonstrates the transformative power of a properly defined and vigorously pursued goal.

Leadership that is founded on a compelling vision provides firms with a sense of direction. Teams collaborate to achieve a single objective, which combines their efforts and propels them forward with zeal. It inspires people to push over their limitations and work toward a more rewarding future.

Creativity: Fueling the Engine of Innovation

While vision sets the objective, creativity drives the innovation engine that propels enterprises forward. Innovative leaders understand that in order to succeed, they must journey into new areas and create novel solutions to difficult problems. They promote unique thinking and new ideas in an environment that advances creativity.

Walt Disney, the brilliant mind behind The Walt Disney Company, is the epitome of a leader who harnessed innovation through the power of imagination. Disney's commitment to aesthetic excellence was nothing short of visionary, bringing to life timeless characters like Mickey Mouse and paving the way for groundbreaking animated masterpieces like "Snow White and the Seven Dwarfs," Steamboat Willie," and "Pinocchio." His unwavering quest to stretch the boundaries of entertainment blossomed like a fairy tale, transforming the business. Disney's limitless imagination and willingness to take artistic risks elevated him to the status of a true trailblazer, leaving an unforgettable imprint on the worlds of animation and storytelling.

Innovative leaders recognize that a diversity of perspectives and ideas is the root of creativity. They promote a welcoming atmosphere in which team members are encouraged to express themselves without fear of being rejected. This collaborative approach forms a rich tapestry of creativity in which many points of view weave together to generate game-changing ideas.

The Symbiosis of Vision & Creativity

Vision and creativity complement one another; they are not mutually exclusive. Vision establishes the goal, and creativity provides the means to realize it. Leaders who capitalize on this mutually beneficial relationship have the potential to ignite innovation and significant change inside their enterprises. It is critical to remember that a vision without a plan or roadmap is merely a wish. Visionaries must set forth the blueprints for others to create or produce the vision. The harmony of vision and creativity may, therefore, genuinely come to life, allowing teams to turn ambitions into reality and move the organization forward.

Steve Jobs, co-founder of Apple Inc., was a real master of combining ingenuity and visionary insight. Jobs orchestrated a symphony of technological marvels to bring his vision to life—a future where technology seamlessly integrated with our daily existence—with an artist's eye for detail and an inventor's enthusiasm. His ingenuity and innovation propelled legendary products such as the iPhone and iPad, which became the cornerstones of a digital revolution. These devices were more than simply gadgets; they were portals to new worlds of creativity, productivity, and connectivity. Jobs etched his name into the annals of history by altering entire sectors and leaving an enduring legacy of invention and advancement, thanks to his unrivaled ability to see the future of technology.

Leaders who place a premium on both vision and creativity inspire creative cultures. They inspire their employees to think creatively, to see big-picture possibilities, and to see beyond the present. This dynamic leadership style elevates the sense of fulfillment among team members who recognize the relevance of their job in the larger picture, in addition to driving growth.

The Characteristics of Visionary Leadership

Visionary leadership demonstrates the ability to imagine and communicate physical, intangible, or even seemingly impossible concepts. Visionaries, such as the well-known polymath Leonardo da Vinci, are distinguished by their ability to envisage as well as map a course for the fulfillment of their aspirations. Leonardo da Vinci's inventiveness extended across several domains, including engineering, science, and the arts. With his ability to imagine flying airplanes and anatomical findings, he laid the groundwork for innovations that would occur decades later. Visionaries must also display an unwavering commitment to identifying problems and, more importantly, finding solutions to them.

They pursue their objectives with unyielding commitment, remaining adaptable, sensitive, and innovative in the face of adversity. Visionaries like conflict because they see it as a means of breaking through complacency and creating an environment receptive to creativity. They truly believe that "if it is conceivable, it is achievable."

Thinking Huge, Thinking Wow

At the center of creating change is the key notion of "Thinking Huge," a revolutionary approach to reenergizing and pushing your team's vision and creativity. As a great leader, there are times when you should focus your attention and resources on large, game-changing initiatives that break the mold and go beyond customary boundaries rather than little, incremental adjustments. This manner of thinking contradicts the cliche "We've always done it this way," and it urges leaders to embrace a mindset that dares to think beyond the box, igniting the spark of creativity and making your efforts stand out.

Don't let other people's fears keep you from taking a risk or trying something new. Think-big leaders inspire their teams to pursue big dreams, strive for difficult goals, and approach problems from unexpected angles, injecting a dose of creativity that elicits a resounding "Wow!" This tactical shift has the potential to generate huge returns on investment, inspire notable and talked-about creativity, break down perceived obstacles conjured up from a place of complacency, and push the team and fellow leaders to previously unimaginable heights of creation and success. Thinking Huge is synonymous with Thinking Wow!

Trending

Great leaders are trendsetters, not trend followers. While remaining current on industry trends is crucial, great leaders don't merely chase popularity; they proactively set the benchmark, becoming pioneers in their field.

Leaders guide their teams into unfamiliar areas, establishing a forward-thinking mentality. They predict future requirements and shape industry trends to their benefit.

Leaders who want to follow trends must alter them rather than duplicate them, bringing their own distinct individuality into the mix. Their objective is not conformity but rather innovation, with trends becoming an extension of their brand's own identity. Mindless fixation with trends and social media, on the other hand, can lead to reactionary behavior that undermines long-term goals. Leaders must be proactive, not reactive. When incorporating trends, it's crucial for leaders to establish clear entrance and exit strategies. This ensures that the adoption of trends aligns with their objectives and remains consistent with their mission and values. The idea is to match trends with the brand, complementing it rather than eroding its character.

Tips & Tricks

1. **Action: Create an Idea Incubator**
   - **Technique:** To implement the "Idea Incubator" program effectively, several actions should be taken. To begin, provide a user-friendly framework for idea submission. Second, establish explicit assessment criteria and designate an idea review committee. Encourage cross-functional cooperation among personnel in various jobs. Finally, assign resources for putting selected ideas into action. This technique allows workers to propose new ideas that are then turned into actionable initiatives for the business.

- **Benefits:** An Idea Incubator program actively encourages employees to engage in creative problem-solving and idea generation. It demonstrates your commitment to creating an atmosphere that encourages new ideas and intrapreneurship.

2. **Action: Borrowing From The Best**
   - **Technique:** Research and study large corporate organizations and dissect the reasoning behind their inventive choices to boost your creativity, especially if you're new to management. Consider how large firms spend billions of dollars on research, design, marketing, and other areas to ensure their success. As an example, consider a marketing scenario. Assume you are a new manager with no expertise who has been charged with preparing a product launch that will include magazine ads. In this circumstance, take a hands-on approach by examining various magazines catering to your target audience. To gain inspiration for your unique ad design, study the ad's features like layout, imagery, messaging, and storytelling that catch your attention, paying attention to the specific colors, their combinations, and how they evoke certain emotions or associations. Study the font choices in these ads and note if they use custom fonts, unique text arrangements, or font sizes to create a distinct visual identity. Examine the imagery and visuals in the ads to identify the types of visuals used, such as photographs, illustrations, or graphics. Look at how they integrate with the overall design and messaging of the ad. Consider the layout and composition, taking note of how elements are arranged, the use of negative space, and the overall balance in the design. Lastly, observe how they convey the product's value and connect with the target audience.
   - **Benefit:** This activity provides novice managers with invaluable insights into the innovation strategy of established organizations. You may employ comparable strategies on

70

your own projects without having to reinvent the wheel if you grasp the "why" behind these creative choices. You may progressively and effectively create your own creative style by learning from these best practices. Understanding the science of corporate creativity may save you time and effort while setting the groundwork for your own creative masterpieces.

3. **Action: Reverse Brainstorming**
    - **Technique:** Using the reverse brainstorming approach, you intentionally generate "bad" or illogical ideas before attempting to convert them into innovative solutions. This technique encourages creative problem-solving and challenges traditional wisdom.
    - **Benefits:** Reverse brainstorming disrupts established thought processes and encourages "outside-the-box" thinking. Teams are given the flexibility to study fresh solutions, resulting in game-changing breakthroughs.
    - **Example**: A retail firm is seeing a significant decrease in foot traffic and sales in its physical locations as a result of increased internet buying.
        i. **Action:** Reverse Brainstorming
            - **Technique:** The team gets together to come up with unusual or "poor" solutions to the decline in foot traffic. Two of the first ideas are listed below:
            1. Make the in-store experience intentionally uncomfortable.
            2. Increase prices to discourage customers from coming to the stores.
            - **Benefits:** Even if the initial ideas appear ludicrous and impractical, the reverse brainstorming process does not end there. The crew is now tasked to transform these unconventional ideas into innovative solutions:

1. Make the in-store experience intentionally uncomfortable.
   a. **Transformation:** Rethink the in-store experience such that it is purposely disruptive in order to capture curiosity and inspire involvement. Create themed, interactive displays that encourage investigation, for example.
2. Increase prices to discourage customers from coming to the stores.
   b. **Transformation:** Use dynamic pricing approaches such as bundling to provide exceptional savings and perks to in-store customers, increasing the attractiveness of the in-store experience.

4. **Action: Employ the Element of Surprise**
   - **Technique:** Sun Tzu urged leaders to utilize surprise as a tool in their leadership. "All men may see these techniques by which I conquer," Sun Tzu advises, "but what none can see is the strategy out of which success is created." Encourage innovation and, on occasion, propose innovative ideas or responses.
   - **Benefit:** Maintaining your team and opponents off-balance promotes a dynamic and creative work environment; according to Sun Tzu's proverb, *"In war, the strategy is to avoid what is powerful and strike at what is weak."* You can disrupt old patterns and study new growth and improvement prospects, resulting in innovative solutions and a competitive edge.

5. **Action: Email Your Creative Sparks**
   - **Technique:** Send yourself a quick email describing your thoughts or ideas anytime you have a creative thought, a moment of inspiration, or come across a scenario that requires a new solution. Include any relevant facts, perceptions, or background that comes to mind.

- **Benefit:** Emailing yourself is a good way to document and save these important thoughts and insights. It provides a specific area to evaluate them later and prevents them from disappearing in the midst of your daily routine or in the middle of the night. This practice promotes creativity and ensures that your initial ideas are not lost by allowing you to expand on these topics when you have more time and attention. It also contributes to the creation of a creative inspiration archive, which you may use whenever you need a fresh perspective or new solutions to difficulties.

6. **Action: Environmental Benchmarking**
   - **Technique:** Examine trends, innovations, and breakthroughs in a variety of fields outside of your sector on a regular basis for you and your team. Encourage discussions on how your company could leverage these outside elements to innovate.
   - **Benefits:** Environmental benchmarking broadens your perspective while also making you aware of new concepts and fashions. It encourages innovative methods and solutions by connecting outside innovations to your company's goals.

7. **Action: Cultivate Curiosity**
   - **Technique:** To promote curiosity, one must actively seek out new knowledge and other points of view. For example, an interested software developer may look at online courses and lectures, scholarly journals, and conferences.
   - **Benefits:** Curiosity promotes creative thinking by encouraging the discovery of new thoughts, connections, and solutions. It broadens your knowledge and encourages creative thinking.

8. **Action: Embrace Diverse Perspectives**
   - **Technique:** Adopting numerous viewpoints requires actively connecting with individuals from other backgrounds and cultures in order to get fresh ideas. A marketing team comprised of employees from several departments, for example, may generate novel and successful marketing approaches by presenting a diversity of viewpoints.
   - **Benefits:** Accepting different viewpoints enhances creativity by exposing you to a wider range of notions and solutions. It promotes diversified thinking and enhances problem-solving strategies.

9. **Action: Mental Reboot**
   - **Technique:** Incorporate methods, such as clearing your thoughts and deep breathing, into your daily routine to generate mental reset periods. If you are feeling pulled in multiple directions at once, take a minute to breathe deeply, exercise mindfulness, and allow your mind to refocus.
   - **Benefits:** The mindful reset method clears your mind of clutter and provides a place for fresh thoughts. Because it reduces stress and distractions, you may approach your task with a new focus, a clear mind, and greater creativity.

10. **Action: Embrace Failure as a Learning Opportunity**
    - **Technique:** Accepting setbacks and failures as chances for progress means viewing these hindrances as possibilities for improvement. For example, a failing company might offer a business owner valuable insight that they can apply to their next venture and help them flourish.
    - **Benefits:** Accepting failure as a learning opportunity encourages exploration and risk-taking, lowering the likelihood of defeat and allowing for more unique and innovative solutions.

11. Action: Encourage a Creative Workspace

- **Technique:** Designing your environment to encourage creativity is an important component of developing a creative workplace. An architect, for example, may build their workspace with large windows that allow in natural light and fill it with tools, artwork, and plants to create a functional but inspiring and comfortable environment.
- **Benefits:** A creative workstation can keep you motivated and engaged by stimulating creativity and enhancing idea development and innovation.

12. Action: Connect Unrelated Concepts

- **Technique:** Making connections between apparently unrelated concepts or disciplines can lead to the development of unexpected solutions. A product designer, for example, may combine industrial design concepts with biomimicry principles to create a more sustainable product.
- **Benefits:** Making connections between seemingly unrelated concepts drives creativity by stimulating "out-of-the-box" thinking, which leads to innovative solutions and fresh views.

Chapter Summary

Vision and imagination are the threads that weave the fabric of transformation. While creativity propels businesses forward with inventive solutions, vision provides a compass direction that guides them toward their future. These variables work together to develop visionary leaders who drive innovation, inspire change, and are disrupters within their businesses. Leaders may effectively traverse the modern world's tough terrain and inspire their teams to achieve remarkable achievements by embracing these visionary attributes.

CHAPTER 7

A-T-P MASTERY:
ADAPTABILITY, TOUGHNESS & PROBLEM SOLVING

Success necessitates adaptability, tenacity, and problem-solving abilities. Leaders who display these characteristics are more than simply managers; they are "doers." This chapter examines the crucial importance of these attributes in leadership, illustrating how they assist CEOs in overcoming challenges, motivating their employees, and leading their organizations to greatness.

The Virtue of Adaptability

Adaptability is the ability to adjust to change with elegance and grace. Leaders who can swiftly shift their methods and perspectives are invaluable assets to their businesses in today's environment where change is the only constant. They see change as an opportunity rather than a danger, and they understand that even the best-laid plans can unravel in the face of unforeseen circumstances.

Take, for example, Satya Nadella's stint as CEO of Microsoft in 2014, which was nothing short of a revolutionary journey. At that critical juncture, Microsoft was at a fork in the road. The company's once-dominant position in the technology industry had been challenged, and it faced strong competition on several fronts. As he oversaw a stunning shift in Microsoft's trajectory, Nadella's adaptability and strategic skill shone brightly.

In a risky move, he shifted the company's focus to the growing fields of cloud computing and artificial intelligence. This strategic shift was nothing short of a revolution, allowing Microsoft to reclaim its relevance and reach new heights. Under Nadella's leadership, the company's market value increased to nearly a trillion dollars, demonstrating the advantages of adaptation and foresight.

The Triumph of Resilience

Resilience, toughness, and tenacity are at the heart of enduring strength. It represents the ability to overcome adversity with enhanced fervor and commitment. Resilient leaders do not falter in the face of adversity because they have their sights set on the long-term goal. They understand that failure is not the end but rather a launching pad for tremendous advancement. Resilient leaders persevere in the face of huge obstacles.

Henry Ford, an automotive legend, is a striking illustration of the force of perseverance forged in the fires of impossible adversity. Ford encountered several challenges along the road, each of which tested his relentless commitment.

Early in his career, Ford had financial difficulties that jeopardized his ambitions. His first effort at a car firm, the Detroit Automobile Company, failed and was closed down. His second business venture, the Henry Ford Company, also failed. Instead of giving up, he used these setbacks to fuel his determination to create a more affordable and accessible vehicle.

Ford's courage was tested when he embarked on the huge job of developing the Model T. The journey was made difficult by technical problems, budgetary restrictions, and the mistrust of industry colleagues. At times, the odds seemed insurmountable.

In the face of these huge hurdles, Ford's determination shined the brightest. His boundless energy and endless commitment to creation enabled him to create the Model T, an industry-changing invention that also changed the course of history.

Henry Ford's life is a fascinating illustration of persistence as a dominant force in leadership. His authority stemmed from his capacity to overcome adversity as well as his track record of achievement. Ford's life exemplifies how strong leaders can thrive despite adversity and convert insurmountable obstacles into chances for greatness.

Solving Problem Solving

Leaders are inherently problem solvers. They thrive when presented with difficult situations that require innovative answers. It is critical to be able to assess problems, identify their roots, and devise feasible remedies. Leaders who can handle issues do not avoid obstacles; in fact, they gravitate towards them.

Jeff Bezos, the founder of Amazon, is a fantastic example. Bezos is known for his relentless search for novel solutions to difficult problems. He revolutionized the e-commerce industry, seeing Amazon as the "everything shop." His attention to overcoming logistical challenges, such as same-day delivery, and his willingness to invest in cutting-edge technology, such as Kindle, indicate his ability to solve problems. Bezos' track record reveals how closely strong leadership and a relentless commitment to problem-solving are linked.

The Symbiotic Relationship

Adaptability, resilience, and problem-solving abilities are not separate attributes but are inextricably intertwined. An adaptive leader has the courage to deal with change as well as the problem-solving skills to capitalize on it. A resilient leader uses their adaptability to overcome obstacles via innovative problem-solving. Effective problem-solving leaders understand that flexibility and resiliency are required for long-term, transformational growth.

Tips & Tricks

1. **Action: Crisis Preparedness & Contingency Planning**
   - **Technique:** Great leaders take the initiative to prepare for disasters and crises. They anticipate potential challenges and have solid backup plans in place to cope with them. These plans include clear roles and responsibilities, communication rules, risk-reduction strategies, and resource sourcing.
   - **Benefits:** Crisis preparation lowers the effect of unanticipated issues and supports leaders in responding quickly and efficiently. It reduces disruptions and strengthens confidence among team members and stakeholders, demonstrating a leader's ability to cope with adversity.

2. **Action: Effective Time Management**
   - **Technique:** Resilient leaders are masters of time management. They employ tools and methods to prioritize activity, set appropriate deadlines, and avoid overextending oneself. They reduce stress and provide a more disciplined work environment for their colleagues by effectively managing their time.
   - **Benefits:** Leaders who manage their time well may focus on critical goals without becoming exhausted. It sets a good example for their employees and encourages better time management skills throughout the organization. As a consequence, productivity and work-life balance improve.

3. **Action: Embrace Technology & Automation**
    - **Technique:** Use automation and technology to speed up operations and reduce the likelihood of human mistakes. Invest in data analysis, reporting, repetitive processes, automation devices, and software. Utilize the metrics and data to dissect and enhance your production, efficiency, and growth.
    - **Benefits:** Technology and automation make tasks more efficient, accurate, and consistent. They provide team members and leaders with additional time and mental capacity to tackle demanding work and adapt to changing circumstances.

4. **Action: Embrace Change & Adaptability**
    - **Technique:** Great leaders understand that change is unavoidable in today's fast-paced world. They don't simply tolerate change; they embrace it as an opportunity for growth and creativity. They remain adaptive and flexible, willing to shift direction when required. This is specifically advantageous when their predecessors chose not to embrace change.
    - **Benefits:** Leaders who embrace change and adaptation are better equipped to respond quickly to shifting circumstances, seize new opportunities, and sustain a competitive edge. It encourages continuous development by cultivating an innovative and creative culture inside the organization.

5. **Action: Make It Right**
    - **Technique:** When confronted with recurring difficulties or obstacles that have persisted due to complexity, time limits, resource restrictions, or simply because "We've always done it this way," adopt the mantra "Make It Right." Take the initiative and confront these issues like a great leader. Break

down the issues into simple stages, allocate work, and use your team's combined strength to create solutions.

- **Benefit:** By acting, you demonstrate your dedication to problem-solving and motivate your staff to do the same. Taking care of chronic issues not only removes bottlenecks but also enhances team morale and efficiency. This method encourages a proactive problem-solving culture and develops an environment in which difficulties are faced with determination rather than avoidance.

6. **Action: Adopt a Growth Mindset**
   - **Technique:** Encourage the idea that talents and intellect can be developed through hard work and perseverance. Encourage ongoing learning for yourself and your team, with an emphasis on perseverance in the face of adversity. Provide educational opportunities mentoring, and set a good example of constant learning and adaptability, instilling in workers a culture of creativity and flexibility.
   - **Benefits:** A growth mindset can help to further a culture of continuous learning and progress. It inspires individuals to embrace obstacles, learn from setbacks, and keep striving for their goals. This method enables personal and organizational progress.

7. **Action: Build a Supportive Network**
   - **Technique:** Recognize the significance of strong support systems. Seek out colleagues, mentors, and advisers who can provide direction, constructive critique, and emotional support at difficult times. Encourage your staff to create their own support networks, creating an environment where help and shared learning are highly appreciated.
   - **Benefits:** Creating a strong support network offers guidance, constructive feedback, and emotional backup during adverse times. It promotes learning, collaboration,

and resilience within teams, opening doors to new opportunities for personal and professional growth.

8. **Action: Develop Stress Management Skills**
   - **Technique:** Stress management should be prioritized as a critical component of resilience. Invest in awareness, regular exercise, effective time management, and relaxation techniques. Prioritize self-care to ensure emotional and physical resiliency. To promote your team's well-being, provide stress-relief tools and create stress-reduction activities.
   - **Benefits:** Leaders may employ stress management tactics to stay on target, make educated decisions, and keep their health in good shape during challenging times. As a consequence, they are better able to control their teams' tension and lead with composure.

9. **Action: Learn from Failure and Setbacks**
   - **Technique:** Resilient leaders see failures and setbacks as opportunities for learning rather than insurmountable obstacles. They analyze what went wrong, revise their strategies, and use failure as a springboard for future success.
   - **Benefits:** Learning from failure and setbacks may help leaders become more resilient and flexible. It leads to greater decision-making, improved problem-solving abilities, and a culture that encourages innovation and risk-taking.

10. **Action: Effective Communication & Transparency**
    - **Technique:** Though seemingly a basic concept, many leaders fail to implement this basic concept properly. Direct and honest communication is vital at all times, but especially during times of uncertainty or disruption. Resilient leaders enlighten their staff and provide reasons and context for

actions. They respond to issues and maintain open channels of contact.

- **Benefits:** Through good communication, team members gain trust and confidence. It reduces ambiguity and anxiety, allowing the team to react to changing situations more efficiently. It also encourages open communication, which will enable leaders to gather insightful recommendations and critiques.

11. Action: Set Clear Goals & Priorities

- **Technique:** Leaders who are resilient prioritize their work and create SMART (Specific, Measurable, Achievable, Relevant, Time-bound) goals. They make certain that their employees are informed of the company's goals and may coordinate their efforts properly. Provide specific roadmaps for accomplishing these goals as necessary to guarantee compliance, efficiency, and logistical coordination. Leaders provide a framework for their teams to work successfully towards achievement by making objectives explicit, measurable, achievable, relevant, and time-bound.

- **Benefit:** SMART objectives provide clarity, accountability, and motivation. They assist people and teams with understanding exactly what is anticipated, how success is measured, and the timelines involved. This method improves attention and efficiency while decreasing ambiguity and misunderstanding. It eventually leads to increased productivity and goal achievement.

Chapter Summary

In the fast-paced world of leadership, the capacity to adapt, be tough, and solve challenges is essential. Leaders who display these characteristics are more than simply managers; they are visionaries. This chapter investigates the crucial importance of these attributes in leadership, illustrating how they assist CEOs in overcoming challenges, motivating their employees, and leading their organizations to greatness. The value of flexibility is emphasized, highlighting how leaders who can swiftly adapt their plans and perspectives are valuable assets to their businesses and may perceive change as an opportunity. While issue resolution is depicted as the foundation of effective leadership, resilience is described as the ability to rebound from adversity. These characteristics are not mutually exclusive; adaptive leaders gain strength from resilience and use problem-solving to create significant change. The chapter finishes with tips for developing these traits, highlighting their transformational influence on leadership and organizational success.

CHAPTER 8

COURAGEOUS LEADERSHIP:
BUILDING CONFIDENCE & RESOLVING CONFLICT

Some characteristics stand out as critical success necessities in the complicated fabric of leadership. Courage, confidence, and conflict resolution are the basic attributes that distinguish outstanding leaders from others. This chapter examines the profound importance of these attributes in leadership, as well as how they enable leaders to take risks, develop trusting relationships, and nurture calm and successful workplaces.

The Essence of Courage: Abraham Lincoln's Fearless Leadership

Outstanding leadership is founded on bravery, which allows individuals to confront danger, uncertainty, and adversity front on. Genuine bravery, on the other hand, goes beyond simply displaying self-control; it also requires the fortitude to face external forces, notably others' fears and doubts.

Leaders with steadfast bravery are typically surrounded by skeptics and cynics. These voices, despite their good intentions, may cast doubt on even the most ambitious efforts. True bold leaders, conversely, persist on their chosen path, unafraid of the uncertainties of others.

Abraham Lincoln, the 16th President of the United States, is seen as a model of courageous leadership. During his presidency, one of the most brutal periods in American history ensued: the Civil War. Lincoln had to deal with the continuous doubts and concerns of those around him, as well as the immense task of preserving the Union.

Many questioned his ability to lead the country during such trying circumstances. Despite this, Lincoln led the United States through its darkest periods because of his tenacity, unbreakable determination, and belief in the ideas of liberty and equality. In a divided society, his leadership provided a vision of optimism.

Abraham Lincoln's life exemplifies how brave leaders not only overcome their own anxieties but also inspire people around them to do the same. Courageous leaders inspire everyone around them by pursuing their mission with zeal and remaining unshakable in the face of adversity. Their bravery becomes a light, guiding their teams and countries over treacherous seas and, in the end, shaping the course of history.

The Power of Confidence: Belief in Self and Vision

Confidence, or unwavering conviction in one's abilities and judgment, is a trait that emanates assurance and inspires others to believe in oneself. It empowers leaders to make solid judgments even when the situation is ambiguous, and it compels their teams to follow.

Leaders who are self-assured have the courage to silence their inner critic, the continuous voice of doubt that may haunt even the most accomplished individuals. They recognize that everyone suffers self-doubt, but they don't let it interfere with their activities or growth. Instead, they rely on their wit and tremendous stores of confidence to overcome hurdles and drive their troops with unshakable determination.

Mary Kay Ash, the founder of Mary Kay Cosmetics, is a superb example of self-assurance in leadership. Mary Kay's journey was distinguished by perseverance, confidence, and a pioneering approach in an industry dominated by men.

Despite the challenges and gender prejudices she encountered, Mary Kay never wavered in her determination to achieve her goals. She saw that self-assurance was not simply a personal trait but also a motivating one that could inspire others. Because of her persistent faith in herself and her ideas, she established a movement and inspired many women to pursue their dreams, overcome challenges, and succeed in business.

Mary Kay Ash's life is a testament to the transformational power of leadership confidence. Her authority came not from a lack of doubt but from her unshakeable belief that she could overcome it and achieve exceptional success. She reminds us that confidence is a quality that may assist us in overcoming challenges, illuminating the path to achievement, and motivating others around us.

Conflict Resolution: Inspired by the "Art of War"

Conflict resolution in teams and organizations, as outlined in Sun Tzu's "Art of War," is critical for transforming conflicts into productive solutions rather than continuing hostilities. Sun Tzu's principles emphasize the importance of differentiating between conflict resolution and issue resolution, which necessitates thorough analysis and decisive action. Leaders who embody Sun Tzu's advice approach conflict with confidence, seeking win-win solutions in the same way that Art of War strategists do.

In Sun Tzu's Art of War, he emphasizes effective communication, strategic leadership, diplomacy, empowering teams to handle disputes, and the advancement of project plans. Consider a project team that is experiencing disagreements regarding the project's direction. The team leader who exudes boldness and confidence, pauses everything, encourages open communication, and urges everyone to express their concerns. The team skillfully resolves issues and incorporates varied opinions into their project approach through diligent and courteous communication.

Following Sun Tzu's principles, effective conflict resolution leaders stress knowing their opponents and the context, recognizing the fundamental causes of disagreements and their environmental context. These leaders understand that it is not about winning or losing but about attaining triumph without needless confrontation, creating an atmosphere in which weaknesses may be transformed into strengths. They amicably settle conflicts using intellect and smart thinking, contributing to the organization's overall success.

Tips & Tricks

1. **Action: Encourage Constructive Disagreement**
   - **Technique:** Confident team leaders create an environment in which members feel comfortable expressing differing opinions and engage in meaningful discussions. They recognize that many points of view may enhance innovation and improve decision-making.
   - **Benefits:** Healthy disagreement helps team members to think critically and creatively. It ensures that decisions are well-informed and well-considered. Leaders who are confident are more open to different points of view, which increases the overall quality of decision-making.

2. **Action: Balance Confidence with Humility**
   - **Technique:** While confidence is important, great leaders also have humility. They express thanks for their accomplishments while also being honest about their flaws and mistakes. This combination of confidence and humility is an excellent leadership trait.
   - **Benefits:** When leaders achieve a balance between confidence and humility, they become more approachable and likable. It allows team members to be transparent and admit their flaws without fear of being condemned and

develops a culture of failure learning. This combination eventually strengthens trust and collaboration.

3. **Action: Face Challenges Head-On**
   - **Technique:** Exhibit courage and leadership by not avoiding uncomfortable situations or difficult conversations. Address issues as they arise, taking a proactive approach when faced with challenges and confrontations. Encourage your team to do the same by demonstrating how to approach difficult situations with confidence and problem-solving skills. Create an open and supportive environment in which team members feel comfortable addressing issues as they arise.
   - **Benefits:** Taking care of issues through direct confrontation prevents issues from worsening and allows leaders to devise swift remedies. As team members see their leader's willingness to take on tough tasks, trust rises between them. Courageous leaders inspire their teams to tackle problems together by cultivating a culture of problem-solving and resilience.

4. **Action: Pick Your Battles; The Philosophy of Strategic Retreat**
   - **Technique:** Consider Sun Tzu's instruction to "choose your fights" when needed. When confronted with challenging barriers or adverse situations, consider the issue thoroughly. Consider strategically retiring or reallocating resources to preserve strength, following Sun Tzu's admonition that "the ultimate art of war is to enslave the adversary without fighting."
   - **Benefit:** By understanding strategic engagement and knowing when to select your battles, you may efficiently save critical resources and reassemble with purpose. Following Sun Tzu's proverb, "Opportunities multiply as they are grasped," this technique positions you for long-term success

and ensures your preparedness for future leadership responsibilities.

5. **Action: Serving Others Without Self-Promotion:**
    - **Technique:** Leadership based on service, combined with humility and confidence, is a potent combination. Leaders who sincerely serve their teams emphasize their members' well-being and progress before personal accolades. Actively assist your team members in reaching their objectives by giving direction, resources, and opportunities for advancement. As a team leader, make it your mission to ensure the personal and professional success of every team member by creating an environment in which they can flourish.
    - **Benefits:** Leading by serving provides a sense of fulfillment to both team members and leaders. It promotes commitment, loyalty, and a productive workplace. By sincerely caring about their employees' success, confident leaders encourage and motivate them.

6. **Action: Continuously Expand Your Knowledge**
    - **Technique:** Active learners are self-assured leaders. They make time to learn new skills, whether through formal schooling, self-study, or observing their coworkers. They remain current on market trends and cutting-edge technologies.
    - **Benefits:** Leadership development keeps individuals adaptable and informed. They may utilize it to make sound judgments and inspire their employees with unique ideas. Leaders who are self-assured are seen as specialists in their fields, which boosts their authority and credibility.

7. **Action: Celebrate Achievements, Both Small & Large**
   - **Technique:** Confident leaders celebrate victories, no matter how big or little. They recognize and cherish their team members' efforts and triumphs. Everything from simple acknowledgments to lavish celebrations is possible.
   Benefits: Celebrating victories boosts team spirit and motivation. It helps to build a pleasant and appreciative culture. Confident leaders understand the importance of recognizing and rewarding effort and dedication, which inspires their employees to maintain their high standards.

8. **Action: Embrace Failure as a Learning Opportunity**
   - **Technique:** Instead of being terrified of failure, self-assured leaders view it as a chance to grow. They understand that failures are an unavoidable part of the leadership journey and that each one teaches us something.
   - **Benefits:** Accepting failure helps to build resilience and bravery. It allows leaders to rebound quickly, armed with new knowledge and attitudes. Leaders who embrace this approach are more willing to take measured risks, which results in innovation.

9. **Action: Avoid What is Strong and Strike at What is Weak**
   - **Technique:** The Art of War emphasizes the importance of being adaptable and quick to change your methods and approaches when faced with changing circumstances, echoing Sun Tzu's view that "in war, the way is to avoid what is strong and strike at what is weak," so embrace this principle during conflict.
   - **Benefit:** Quick adaptation makes you relevant and successful in shifting settings, replicating Sun Tzu's statement that "water bends its path according to the character of the land over which it flows." It helps you to manage your team

confidently in the face of uncertainty, capitalize on emerging trends, and successfully adjust to problems.

10. Action: Know Your Opponent

- **Technique:** Confident leaders invest time and effort in understanding the motives, points of view, and concerns of the parties engaged in a conflict, just as Sun Tzu emphasized the significance of knowing your opponent. This information informs their approaches to dispute resolution.

- **Benefits:** Knowing your enemies allows you to anticipate their maneuvers and reactions, making it easier to negotiate agreements and settle problems. Furthermore, it promotes open communication among all parties and demonstrates your commitment to finding win-win solutions.

11. Action: Leverage Allies

- **Technique:** Strong leaders build networks of allies and supporters inside their organization or industry. They can rely on these supporters to provide advice, act as mediators in disputes, or assist them in reaching a settlement when they are in a dispute.

- **Benefits:** Allies can help you expand your dispute resolution options. It promotes collaboration and shared accountability for conflict resolution. Furthermore, it demonstrates your ability to develop and maintain relationships, which is an important leadership attribute.

12. Action: Master the Nuances of Timing

- **Technique:** Timing is critical in resolving disagreements. The most effective leaders understand when to initiate talks, give solutions, and escalate issues. They recognize that waiting for the perfect chance may have a major impact on the outcome.

- **Benefits:** Understanding the nuances of time increases the likelihood of dispute resolution. It helps leaders to seize opportunities, eliminate resistance, and prevent disputes from worsening. Furthermore, it exhibits strategic thought, foresight, and appropriate timing.

13. **Action: Employ Psychological Warfare**
    - **Technique:** Psychological warfare, when used in the context of leadership, refers to the capacity to influence people through persuasive discourse, empathy, and emotional intelligence. Leaders employ methods such as active listening, empathy, and good communication to win disputes.
    - **Benefits:** Psychological warfare makes enemies more susceptible to finding common ground by creating rapport and trust within them. It reduces stress and encourages cooperation, making dispute resolution easier and more effective.

14. **Action: LEAP Approach**
    - **Technique:** The LEAP Approach is particularly useful in resolving workplace conflicts between coworkers or supervisors, mediating disagreements within families, friendship groups, or other social circles, handling customer complaints and professional service conflicts, enhancing relationships by resolving recurring problems and preventing future conflicts, and addressing personal disagreements and misunderstandings in various contexts. The LEAP approach has four major components: Listen, Empathize, Apologize, and Produce.
        - i. **Listen:** Engage all parties in active listening to their concerns, points of view, and feelings. Give them your whole attention, request clarity, and make sure they know you are listening.

    ii. **Empathize:** Put yourself in the shoes of the disputing parties to better comprehend their sentiments and points of view. Demonstrate empathy by acknowledging their feelings when appropriate, repeating their key points, and exhibiting an interest in their experiences.

    iii. **Apologize:** Express your sincere remorse for any errors, misunderstandings, or unpleasant situations that led to the disagreement, if required. Even if it's just to express remorse for having to go through it or be inconvenienced, accepting responsibility may go a long way toward resolving problems.

    iv. **Produce:** Collaborate with the parties to develop ideas and solutions to address the underlying reasons for the conflict. Concentrate on identifying win-win outcomes and long-term strategies. Lastly, follow up with the affected party and let them know that something was done about the issue, whether fully resolved or not.

- **Benefits:** The LEAP approach is good for dispute resolution. Encourage active listening and respect for other points of view to better communication. Empathy establishes trust and increases collaborative problem-solving. Sincere regrets reduce tension and show a wish for peace. The communication of "produced" results communicates that the issue was taken seriously, something was done about it and offers sometimes much-needed closure.

15. Action: Emotionally Intelligent Conflict Resolution

- **Technique:** Begin by acknowledging and appreciating the other person's feelings in a dispute when they are arguing emotionally rather than intellectually. Express empathy through phrases such as, "I can tell that this problem has bothered you" or "I understand that you're feeling passionate about this." Once you've established an emotional connection, gradually steer the conversation toward being more reasonable and solution-focused. Ask open-ended questions to encourage them to express themselves more calmly, and actively listen to them without passing judgment. When it is appropriate (when they are less emotional), enquire about a suitable resolution. Even if you disagree with the answer, it moves the debate from the "complaint phase" to the "solution phase."

- **Benefit:** Emotionally intelligent conflict resolution is a powerful tool for reducing tense situations and finding common ground. Starting the dialogue by acknowledging the other person's sentiments reduces the emotional intensity by making the person feel heard and understood. As the debate progresses toward a more reasonable discussion, it becomes easier to identify the root reasons for the conflict and collaboratively explore viable solutions. Finally, this strategy improves comprehension, empathy, and resolution while also improving collaborative relationships and team dynamics.

16. Action: Sun Tzu's Principle of Winning Without Fighting

- **Technique:** Sun Tzu's principle of "winning without fighting" is reflected by outstanding leaders who, wherever feasible, attempt to resolve differences without resorting to bloodshed. They look for alternatives to direct conflict, such as compromises, concessions, or other methods. Especially when dealing with internal disputes, try to ensure all employees save face, when possible, are not cast as "losers," are united on the resolution, and all have grown from the experience.

- **Benefits:** Workplace disruptions are reduced when conflict is avoided, and harmony is maintained. It indicates your ability to resolve issues politely, which may enhance team spirit. Furthermore, it reduces the emotional toll that conflict has on all sides so future synergies can flourish.

Chapter Summary

The three basic pillars of excellent leadership—courage, confidence, and conflict resolution—all play critical roles in guiding individuals and organizations to success. This chapter focuses on how these characteristics enable leaders to take calculated risks, nurture trust among their teams, and create productive and composed work environments. The chapter discusses the significance of courage and then delves into the power of confidence. Finally, the chapter examines conflict resolution through Sun Tzu's "Art of War," emphasizing the importance of effective communication, strategic leadership, and diplomacy. It provides a set of actionable strategies, such as viewing failure as a learning opportunity, getting to know your opponent, and mastering the nuances of timing to assist leaders in effectively resolving conflicts and fostering productive working relationships.

CHAPTER 9

CULTIVATING COOL, CALM & COLLECTED LEADERSHIP

The ability to remain calm under pressure and preserve objectivity is a trait that defines greatness. This chapter examines the vital need for maintaining calm and avoiding emotional outbursts in leadership.

The Cool & Collected Leader

During the tumultuous years of World War II, Winston Churchill, the indomitable British Prime Minister, was a light of unflinching composure amidst persistent adversity. He exhibited extraordinary poise in the face of continuous and catastrophic bombings, providing strong leadership to his country during its darkest hours. Churchill's unbroken calm became a global image of unrivaled strength and unyielding determination. His iconic image, cigar in hand, addressing the people during air raids, became a timeless emblem of resilience in the face of dire circumstances, leaving an everlasting stamp on the pages of history.

Being composed is vital to competent directing and is more than just a leadership characteristic. A calm leader, such as Churchill, communicates certainty and steadiness, providing the backbone for their team to face issues head-on.

The Dangers of Knee-Jerk Reactions

Effective leadership is doomed by knee-jerk reactions, which are typically motivated by panic, emotional distress, or uncertainty. Hurried answers usually feed the fires of a crisis rather than extinguishing them. Leaders who respond too hastily risk being stuck in a firefighting cycle rather than delivering effective leadership. Such hasty judgments might aggravate the issue and have unexpected effects. Effective leaders like Churchill recognize that quick fixes rarely have long-term benefits.

Objectivity: FDR's Steadfast Leadership

Objectivity serves as a constant guide, lighting the path ahead of us. It comprises the capacity to set aside emotional reactions and view situations objectively and rationally, which is essential when dealing with complicated challenges, strategic decisions, and personnel concerns.

Let's consider Franklin D. Roosevelt's outstanding leadership at a critical point in American history. Under FDR's leadership, the United States faced the dual challenges of the Great Depression and World War II, an era that demanded the greatest impartiality and equanimity.

FDR's extraordinary ability to remain objective in the midst of these turbulent times was a monument of clear-headed, reasoned judgment. His balanced attitude to weathering the economic crisis is an illustration of his objectivity. He advocated for programs such as the New Deal, which intended to alleviate suffering, rebuild a shattered economy, and reform the banking system while retaining fiscal restraint. With a steady hand on the tiller, he expertly managed the country through unprecedented adversity, guiding it to economic recovery and eventual triumph in the worldwide fight. FDR's leadership was a light of steadfast impartiality, serving as a pillar of strength during these difficult times and ultimately leading the country toward a brighter future.

FDR's long-lasting influence demonstrates the value of objectivity in leadership. His continuous dedication to making objective judgments bolstered his authority, proving that even in the face of immense adversity, leaders who choose objectivity illuminate a route to development and perseverance.

The Leadership Ripple Effect

When leaders consistently practice remaining calm, objective, and measured in their responses, their businesses benefit in a variety of ways. This rippling effect can be better understood by considering what occurs when leaders lose their cool. When managers act rashly or succumb to stress in particular situations, it can set a terrible precedent inside the company. Members of the team may see this lack of discipline as an indication that it is okay to behave emotionally rather than intellectually in difficult situations. As a result, a culture of heightened stress, impulsive judgment, and poor leadership may emerge. When leaders, on the other hand, retain their cool in difficult situations, they set a good example for their teams and inspire others to do the same. This promotes a respectful and effective environment, which leads to improved decision-making and team performance.

Tips & Tricks

1. **Action: Time Management**
   - **Technique:** Maintaining a calm, cool, and collected demeanor requires effective time management. Begin by identifying key activities, ranking them based on importance and deadlines, and creating a detailed timetable that allows for proactive preparations as well as unanticipated problems. Make use of time management tools and technologies to improve your planning and overall readiness. To avoid burnout and maintain a good work-life balance, clearly

identify the boundaries between your business and personal lives and make sure your staff is aware of them.

- **Benefit:** Preparing and controlling a comprehensive timeline and allotting contingency time for last-minute concerns allows you to respond to situations coolly and calmly. This acquired respite in the midst of adversity, or looming deadlines enhances your overall resilience and allows you to approach difficulties with a clear and focused viewpoint, ultimately leading to better outcomes.

2. **Action: Comprehensive Contingency Planning**
   - **Technique:** Comprehensive contingency planning requires laboriously preparing for a wide variety of potential issues and emergencies. Recognizing various outcomes, defining reactions to each, and having a well-thought-out strategy ready for implementation are all part of this. This obligation also includes establishing separate roles and duties within your team to carry out these proactive strategies.
   - **Benefit:** This rigorous planning ensures that you are prepared with resources and time to manage adversity with grace and agility, minimizing the impact of unanticipated occurrences on your organization.

3. **Action: Convert Nervous Energy to Active Preparation**
   - **Technique:** Consider any anxiety or apprehension as a signal from your body that you may not be totally prepared for a task or event. Rather than succumbing to your worry, utilize it as an indicator to divert the harmful energy into beneficial action. Spend a few moments examining the root of your concern and identifying how you may better prepare yourself. Use that energy to better your readiness by planning, studying, practicing, or producing.
   Benefit: Channeling anxiousness toward preparedness is revolutionary. It allows you to turn fear into a powerful

instrument for personal development. By actively addressing the reasons for your fear and taking real measures to enhance your preparation, you can strengthen your confidence and increase your chances of success. By participating in this exercise, you may control your anxiety in a proactive manner and increase your capacity to deal with problems efficiently and calmly.

4. **Action: Encourage Controlled Risk-Taking**
   - **Technique:** Encourage your team to take appropriate risks while emphasizing the importance of learning from errors and losses. Allow team members to propose and implement cutting-edge ideas, even if they are risky. As an example, consider the controlled burn approach, which firefighters use to learn to combat wildfires efficiently. They purposely set controlled flames in order to study fire behavior, develop strategies, and enhance their firefighting abilities.
   - **Benefits:** By promoting appropriate risk-taking, a culture of creativity and self-assurance is promoted. Your team will be given the flexibility to actively seek opportunities for growth and improvement while learning valuable lessons from both successes and failures. Your team may develop new skills and procedures by taking calculated risks, much as firefighters use controlled burns to improve their performance. This method may result in game-changing ideas and continued development inside your organization.

5. **Action: Continuous Scenario Testing**
   - **Technique:** Conduct scenario testing sessions on a regular basis to gauge and guide your team's reaction strategies in simulated crisis circumstances. Use these to identify preliminary markers that may indicate forthcoming issues, common reactionary mistakes, resource limitations, and exit strategies.

- **Benefits:** Making crisis management a routine part of your team's job through ongoing scenario testing boosts their confidence and preparedness. It ensures that your employees remain calm and efficient in the face of serious issues.

6. **Action: Gather Intel**
   - **Technique:** Obtaining exact and comprehensive information is critical during times of crisis. Previously established effective two-way communication pathways between the micro and macro environments are crucial for the swift and efficient reception of information. Verifying the reliability of newly sourced information is also essential, especially in this day and age of widespread disinformation on social media. Refrain from making hasty decisions until you have verified any unsubstantiated information.
   - **Benefit:** Incorrect or inadequate data can lead to poor decision-making and stress. With the proper communication channels from vetted and reliable sources in place prior to any situation, you will make better judgments and enhance your crisis management abilities, perhaps reducing the crisis's impacts.

7. **Action: Effective Communication**
   - **Technique:** Maintaining solid communication channels is critical during times of crisis. This necessitates paying close attention to those around you and successfully and concisely articulating your thoughts. Communicate through a variety of means, such as technology and timely meetings, and employ planned communication strategies like communiqués and press releases. Ensure you have defined tasks and roles for each team member according to their abilities and responsibilities. Grant appropriate authority with tasked responsibilities.

- **Benefit:** Effective communication increases your ability to manage emergencies by improving cooperation, decreasing stress levels, and encouraging problem-solving inside your organization. By assigning clear duties and creating deadlines for communication action items, you can ensure that information is provided as soon as possible, reducing the potential for friction and conflicts. Effective communication benefits include improved team collaboration, reduced stress and disturbances, improved problem-solving, and improved outcomes in dealing with a variety of situations and problems.

8. **Action: Don't Them See You Sweat**
   - **Technique:** Emotional regulation refers to your ability to identify and master your emotions, particularly in stressful situations. This includes methods like concentrating solely on the current task at hand, staying organized, and retaining control over the decision-making process. When stress-induced emotion begins to build up, employ methods such as positive self-talk and taking short breaks to compose oneself. Stay positive and focused at all times, especially when confronted with adverse information. Acknowledge the new information as that, just new information. Use it to adapt your strategy and move on.
   - **Benefits:** Whatever the scenario, your ability to regulate your emotions will help you to stay cool and collected, avoiding emotional outbursts, impulsive responses, and displaying fear or insecurity, all of which can impair your ability to make decisions and communicate with others. This promotes better communication and leads to more rational and well-thought-out decision-making. In the end, encouraging a healthy work environment and constructive interactions within your team and stakeholders boosts your effectiveness as a leader.

9. **Action: Positive Self-Talk & Resilience**

  - **Technique:** Increase your confidence and relaxation by using uplifting affirmations and positive self-talk. Create a helpful inner mantra that reminds you of your abilities to overcome obstacles. In addition to engaging in a positive self-talk approach, another effective way to increase resilience is to include constructive self-scrutiny or the "devil's advocate" mindset into your thought process. Use this strategy to carefully examine opposing opinions, prospective obstacles, and difficult circumstances in your internal dialogue. By recognizing and resolving these opposing viewpoints, you may strengthen your confidence and decision-making, ensuring you are well-prepared to face unforeseen problems.

  - **Benefit:** Resilience and positive self-talk increase your mental toughness, giving you the certainty and growth-minded attitude, you need to handle issues. It reminds you that you have been through tough times before and have always come out of it ahead. Adversity shapes and sculpts leaders; embrace it as a badge of mental honor rather than succumbing to a victim mentality.

10. **Action: Ask For Help**

  - **Technique:** When faced with issues, don't be reluctant to seek advice or help from coworkers, mentors, or trustworthy friends. It is not a sign of weakness to turn off your ego. Reach out to others regarding your situation to gain valuable insights, fresh perspectives, access to resources, and reassurance.

  - **Benefit:** Seeking help gives you access to a larger pool of information, decreases stress, encourages inventive problem-solving, and expands your network, all of which contribute to greater resilience in leadership situations.

Chapter Summary

What differentiates leadership excellence is evident: the capacity to stay calm, remain unshakable, and be objective in stressful situations. This chapter highlights the need to remain calm and refrain from impulsive acts when leading people. It underlines how staying cool and composed under duress is not only a leadership characteristic but a critical component of effective leadership. Such an attitude emanates confidence and steadfastness, allowing teams to face challenges with tenacity. The chapter also explores the consequences of rash judgments and underlines the critical role of objectivity in leadership, demonstrating its ability to effect considerable change. The Leadership Ripple Effect is also discussed, in which leaders consistently show calm, impartiality, and measured responses, benefiting their organizations and themselves.

Section II

Crafting Your Leadership Style

Welcome to Section II: Developing Your Leadership Style, where we will continue to hone your leadership skills. We delve into the art of leadership, analyzing the aspects that distinguish your individual style, much like a craftsman stamping his personal brand on his work. From leading by example, where you become the pattern for excellence, to adopting resilience and thick skin, the warrior's armor against hardship, there is no better way to prepare for adversity. We'll look at ways to inject energy and vigor into your leadership, giving you a competitive advantage. We'll also look at the value of approachability leadership in the era of empathy and how humor can help you be more effective. As we embark on the journey of exploring leadership principles, let's make a metaphorical toast to crafting a leadership style as distinctive as a masterpiece.

CHAPTER 10

LEADING BY EXAMPLE:
THE BLUEPRINT FOR OUTSTANDING LEADERSHIP

Setting the example is more than just a technique for genuinely inspirational leaders; it is a way of life. In this chapter, we set out to understand the important consequences of leading by example in all areas of leadership.

Inspiration and Trust

Leadership is based on inspiration, and those who lead by example have a unique ability to motivate and inspire trust in their people. Their actions speak louder than their words, encouraging those they lead to strive for excellence. Consider Mahatma Gandhi, who led India to independence via peaceful civil disobedience. Millions of others were inspired by his personal commitment to peaceful protest and selflessness to follow in his footsteps and strive for a better future.

Credibility is established through trust, and team members cultivate trust when they emulate your example. Leaders who practice what they preach, driven by sincerity, nurture trust at its core.

Leadership's Triad: Aligning, Accountability, & Efficiency

Consider three factors that contribute to leadership success: alignment, accountability, and efficiency.

Alignment, which acts as a compass, directs the organization's path. Aligned leaders ensure that their actions always match the company's morale beliefs and objectives. This alignment creates a clear and defined direction, ensuring that everyone in the company develops together.

Accountability surfaces as the weighing scale measuring the commitment and responsibility of the leader's ability to lead individuals and groups toward success. When employees witness their boss accept responsibility for their own actions, they are inspired to do the same, setting a foundation of accountability for the organization.

Efficiency is the organization's turbo boost, propelling it ahead toward its goals. Setting a good example here often results in increased effectiveness and productivity. Workers are driven to match this pace by their leader's consistent work ethic and devotion. Thus, the organization develops with increasing energy and effectiveness.

The Multifaceted Impact of Leading by Example

Setting a positive example for others has a wide-ranging influence on all aspects of organizational life. Leaders who set an example of ethical and polite behavior are effective negotiators when it comes to settling conflicts and maintaining a positive workplace culture. Leaders who prioritize self-care and work-life balance set the standard for well-being, minimizing burnout, and increasing overall morale. Furthermore, promoting employee well-being is critical to maintaining a healthy and successful team. Having a motivated and content workforce benefits not just the individual employees but also the company's success.

Innovation thrives when leaders display creativity and risk-taking. Elon Musk, the visionary entrepreneur of SpaceX and Tesla, pushes the frontiers of innovation by encouraging experimentation and creativity among his staff. This establishes an environment in which new ideas can emerge. Leaders who lead by example in this realm also inspire staff development by providing an example of constant learning and self-improvement which creates a culture of growth and advancement. They encourage team members to engage in their own development, creating an environment in which staff are always learning and adapting to new challenges. Furthermore, organizations with leaders who lead by example have greater worker retention and recruiting rates. Employees are more likely to stay with a business if they respect and like the actions of their boss.

Be Happy

Being happy at work is an important component of leading by example. The attitude and manner of a leader have a significant impact on the entire work environment and the morale of their team. It's unrealistic to expect team members to be happy and motivated if the leader is not. Leaders who exhibit positivity, enthusiasm, and contentment at work provide a great example for their staff, demonstrating to them that work can be a source of fulfillment and joy. As a result, the workplace can become more engaging and productive.

Creating a pleasant workplace in which team happiness is a shared duty is a full-time job in and of itself. The leader of such a workforce must establish a culture of mutual respect, trust, and support among team members. This means that individuals see that their own well-being is intertwined with the well-being of their colleagues and the team's overall performance. Leaders urge team members to take control of their workplace dynamics by promoting the idea of leaving their personal drama at the door and ensuring that everyone contributes to a positive atmosphere.

Furthermore, a leader's role is to set the tone for the entire team by modeling professionalism and productivity. Leaders support the idea that work should be a place of professional progress and achievement by leading by example and leaving their own drama at the door while remaining focused on the task at hand. Great leaders demonstrate that they can handle problems with a pleasant, warm, and welcoming approach, maintaining a cheerful work environment regardless of the challenges or crises that may happen. Finally, by continually exhibiting contentment and a good attitude, leaders set the bar for their team, fostering a culture in which happiness and productivity are the ultimate goals for all employees.

No Excuses

A major part of leading by example is the concept of "no excuses." Effective leaders recognize that challenges and obstacles will always exist in any undertaking, but they are convinced that there is a solution to every problem. They operate on the premise that no matter what the conditions are, there is always a method to complete the task at hand or adapt to the situation. This mindset promotes a proactive and solution-oriented approach in which leaders and their teams collaborate to develop creative and practical solutions to whatever challenges they may face.

A key aspect of "no excuses" leadership is meeting deadlines and responsibilities with forthright commitment. Leaders who adopt this mindset not only set clear expectations but also guarantee that they meet or even exceed those standards on a consistent basis. If it becomes clear that a deadline cannot be fulfilled for any reason, these leaders prioritize communication. They reach out well in advance to discuss the situation, providing valid arguments and, if necessary, alternate options. This approach exhibits accountability and integrity, demonstrating that they take their obligations seriously and value their team members' time and efforts. They demonstrate that they are not willing to play the victim and instead take charge, demonstrating that they are thoroughly committed to getting the job done.

Overachievement Reexamined

Why have overachievers, at times, earned such an undeservedly negative reputation? Overachievers are the driving force behind exceptional leadership. These individuals are not satisfied with simply meeting expectations; they continually exceed them, often doing more than their share, and creating a high bar for their teams to follow. They lead by example, demonstrating that stretching one's boundaries and exceeding the limits are not only possible but necessary in the quest for greatness. Overachievement in leadership is not about outdoing others or even perfectionism; it's about encouraging and motivating others to adopt a similar mindset, break away from mediocrity, and produce amazing achievements.

Tips & Tricks

1. **Action: Personal-Professional Boundary Reinforcement**
    -   **Technique:** Set a good example for others to follow by keeping personal and professional concerns separate. Avoid bringing personal concerns or outside turmoil to work, and always maintain a professional demeanor.
    -   **Benefit:** This strategy sets a strong precedence for your employees, emphasizing the importance of professionalism and attention to detail in the workplace. By keeping personal concerns out of the office, you promote a more effective and productive work environment, as well as making yourself and your team more approachable and mindful of one another's time. It motivates your employees to follow suit, promoting a collaborative and task-focused working culture.

2. **Action: Taking Ethical Actions: Upholding Ethical Values**
    -   **Technique**: Being truthful is simply one component of demonstrating integrity; another is consistently adhering to

115

moral and ethical norms. This entails always behaving morally, even when no one is looking. Leaders can utilize this approach by applying ethical discernment and ensuring that their conduct aligns with the principles they profess. For example, if a leader values openness, they should communicate and share information with their team in a way that promotes trust. Integrity-based leadership builds credibility and establishes a high moral standard for the group to emulate.

- **Benefit:** When a company has a culture of trust and ethical behavior, it strengthens the acceptance of similar values and increases trustworthiness and respect amongst its team.

3. **Action: Work Ethic: Setting the Standard**
   - **Technique:** Setting high standards for yourself and your team in terms of dedication and work ethic is a critical component of leading by example. Leaders can utilize this if they consistently demonstrate dedication to activities and projects. When leaders consistently meet deadlines, are always at the right place and the right time, steadily go above and beyond, and always arrive on time, the team understands what is expected of them.
   - **Benefit:** When the team leader sets a high standard for work ethic and dedication, the team is driven to consistently perform at their best, creating a work climate in which everyone is committed to achieving established goals.

4. **Action: Cultivate Sportsmanship**
   - **Technique:** A resilient leader cultivates sportsmanship by personally emphasizing the importance of graciousness in both victory and defeat. The leader exemplifies this behavior by recognizing the efforts of team members, competitors, and collaborators regardless of the outcome. At the same time, they consistently demonstrate leadership by actively

participating in tasks, upholding ethical standards, and demonstrating a strong commitment to the organization's mission.

- **Benefit:** The leader's dual approach of cultivating sportsmanship and leading by example creates a positive and inclusive environment. By acknowledging victories with humility and defeats with resilience, the leader builds trust and camaraderie within the team. This strategy encourages team members to embrace difficulties, learn from failures, and strive for continual development.

5. **Action: Positivity in Practice: Overcoming Challenges with Optimism**
   - **Technique:** Positivity is vital for overcoming hurdles and establishing a productive work environment. Leaders may exploit this by adopting a positive attitude about issues and proposing solutions rather than dwelling on them. They can act as role models by gracefully and resiliently embracing failure.
   - **Benefit:** Positive thinking in action increases flexibility, ingenuity, and problem-solving abilities in team members, promoting a creative and innovative work atmosphere.

6. **Action: Embracing Growth: Continuous Learning in Action**
   - **Technique:** Leaders dedicated to continuous learning actively pursue opportunities for professional and personal improvement while motivating their staff to do the same. Seek out workshops, seminars, webinars, or courses that can help you learn new things. Accept mentoring and seek advice from professionals in your industry. Encourage your team to begin on their own learning journeys as well. Encourage their involvement in training programs, seminars, and courses that are relevant to their responsibilities and career goals.

- **Benefit:** By actively embracing growth via continuous learning, a culture of innovation, adaptability, and better problem-solving abilities is formed, which adds to the organization's expansion and success.

7. **Action: Effective Communication in Motion**
   - **Technique:** Effective communication is the cornerstone of any successful team. To ensure clear communication, it is critical to listen to the speaker actively, demonstrating understanding through engaged body language and clarifying questions when necessary, using plain and straightforward language, and encouraging feedback from the receiver to ensure that the message has been accurately understood.
   - **Benefit:** Effective communication in motion promotes accurate team performance and goal attainment by increasing transparency, cooperation, and alignment.

8. **Action: Taking Ownership: Cultivating Accountability**
   - **Technique:** Leaders who accept responsibility for their actions and decisions build an accountability culture throughout their teams. Admitting mistakes and taking measures to set things right is what responsibility requires. Leaders may take advantage of this by assuming responsibility for their actions and being upfront about the outcomes of their decisions.
   - **Benefit:** Accountability and ownership foster effective problem-solving, a trusting culture, and a feeling of obligation among team members, all of which contribute to organizational success.

9. **Action: Empathy and Respect: Nurturing Harmony**
   - **Technique:** Nobody likes a boss that is a bully. Respect and empathy are critical for creating a pleasant work

environment. Leaders may employ this by treating team members with fairness, kindness, and care. They must appreciate diverse perspectives and actively seek to understand the needs and motivating factors of their stakeholders and team members.

- **Benefit:** Promoting respect and empathy in the workplace promotes relationships, teamwork, and collaboration, resulting in a more productive and pleasant workplace with higher employee retention and recruiting prowess.

Chapter Summary

Setting a positive example is a tremendous force in the complex realm of leadership. For truly inspirational leaders, it transcends basic strategy and becomes a way of life. This chapter embarks on an exploration of its profound impact on several areas of leadership. It emphasizes the crucial role of leaders who set a strong example, as their actions speak volumes and uniquely inspire and motivate their teams. Trust and credibility are also enhanced when leaders do what they teach and encourage authenticity. This chapter also delves into the three pillars of leadership—alignment, accountability, and efficiency—and explains how setting a good example demonstrates these characteristics within the group. It also examines the many varied benefits of leading by example, such as how it affects retention, innovation, conflict resolution, and staff growth.

CHAPTER 11

RESILIENCE & THICK SKIN:
THE WARRIOR'S ARMOR

Having "Thick Skin" is a management characteristic that usually emerges as the unsung hero of leadership success. This unique characteristic enables managers to handle the intricacies of their profession with elegance and grace, allowing them to rise above criticism, avoid taking things personally, and the ability to assess issues objectively. In this chapter, we will look at the benefits of managing with resilience and objectivity while shifting attention away from meaningless drama and into the realm of inventive problem-solving.

Embracing Resilience in the Managerial Odyssey

Meet Sachiko, a capable manager in charge of a diverse workforce in the growing hotel business. As she navigates the continuously shifting currents of her profession, Sachiko faces a flurry of obstacles, including client complaints, staff disagreements, and operational issues. Her hidden weapon, though, is her thick skin, a warrior's shield forged by experience and wisdom.

Sachiko displays resilience, or the ability to recover from setbacks while remaining calm and determined. She understands that not all critiques are personal slights and that challenges are opportunities for personal growth. Rather than succumbing to negativity, she directs her energy into issue-solving. Her workforce is inspired by her ability to confront challenges head-on and focus on finding solutions.

The Guiding Light of Objectivity

The impartiality of objectivity is a guiding principle. It includes taking a step back, detaching oneself from one's emotional tendencies, and assessing situations logically. This characteristic comes in handy when managing human behaviors, analyzing performance, or making key decisions. When you shift your viewpoint to perceive issues and obstacles as pure learning opportunities, you open yourself to a wealth of information and opportunities for progress.

Consider the situation in which a manager is required to report to an ineffective supervisor. Learning from a poor employer may be just as, if not more, instructive than learning from a good one. These inept leaders can teach us valuable lessons about what we should avoid in positions of leadership. Their management tactics and behaviors can egregiously demonstrate the harmful impacts of undesirable attributes such as micromanagement, poor communication, partiality, bullying, and others.

By closely objectively examining the weaknesses of subpar employers, you can obtain essential insights into becoming a better leader. By following this approach, you may avoid their mistakes and develop a leadership style that is both successful and empathetic, generating a positive work atmosphere and assisting your team's progress. Furthermore, this approach can help transform challenging situations into valuable lessons for personal growth, reducing frustrations and boosting morale as you gain vital insights to improve your own leadership style and build a positive work environment that aids your team's advancement.

Transformation Through Problem-Solving Leadership

The concept of problem-solving leadership is central to effective management. True leaders enjoy developing solutions and accelerating progress. They understand that their job entails more than simply identifying problems; it also entails steering the ship toward solutions and advancements.

Consider Joseph, a department head of a large firm that has to implement a cutting-edge workflow system. Instead of succumbing to despair, Joseph embarks on a cooperative journey. He gathers feedback from his team, finds problem areas, evaluates viable remedies, acquires resources, creates a solid roadmap and timeline, and handles the transition seamlessly. Joseph's devotion to problem-solving develops team trust in addition to guaranteeing a seamless transition.

The Positive Perception Paradox

Perception has enormous power: perception is reality. A negative attitude about obstacles can lead to mental and physical exhaustion, which can eventually diminish motivation. A positive attitude, on the other hand, can turn problems into possibilities, causing pleasure and even releasing endorphins, the body's natural mood boosters. This burst of optimism inspires leaders to strive for and accomplish even more, creating a vicious cycle of productivity.

Consider a manager who is dealing with budgetary restrictions. A gloomy view may create irritation and worry, harming not only their own well-being but also that of their colleagues. However, a positive mindset reframes the financial limits as a blank canvas for innovative cost-cutting or revenue-generating solutions that may even open up new avenues for advancement. This adjustment in perspective enhances confidence, develops a motivational loop, and feeds a hunger for innovative resolution.

Understanding Endorphins and Cortisol for Resilient Leadership

Endorphins, also known as "feel-good" hormones, play an important role in shaping a manager's attitude and, as a result, growth by acting as natural mood boosters. However, it is critical to recognize their counterpart, cortisol, also known as the stress hormone, can test even the most resilient leaders.

The Role of Endorphins

When resilience and an optimistic outlook are maintained, endorphins are released, lessening the impact of stress and negative thinking. Resilient leaders experience an endorphin surge when faced with adversity. This biological response fuels their motivation to maintain a positive attitude, setting in motion a cycle of emotional resilience. Overcoming challenges that may have seemed insurmountable initially provides them with a profound sense of accomplishment, bolstering their courage to confront future obstacles.

The Impact of Cortisol

Cortisol, on the other hand, is released in response to a range of stresses, including physical, emotional, and psychological causes. Physical stress can be caused by strenuous physical activity, illness, accident, or trauma. Anxiety, fear, anger, or despair are examples of emotional stressors, whereas psychological stress is caused by high-pressure circumstances, work-related stress, and personal issues. Inadequate sleep, poor diet, and an excessive intake of coffee or stimulants can all lead to increased cortisol levels. Chronic stress, whether from constant professional pressures or ongoing personal issues, can result in prolonged increases in cortisol production.

Understanding the interaction between endorphins and cortisol is critical for leaders seeking to acquire the resilience and emotional fortitude required to face leadership difficulties. Leaders may acquire the thick skin and resiliency necessary to flourish in their professions by leveraging the power of endorphins and efficiently regulating cortisol levels.

Tips & Tricks

1. **Action: Emotional CrossFit: Toughening Leadership Resilience**
   - **Technique:** Effective leadership requires a strong exterior, one that can accept or reject criticism without internalizing it. Consider it a type of emotional CrossFit in which you strengthen your fortitude like a muscle. Turning your emotions on and off is similar to working out with weights. When confronted with criticism or disappointment, take a step back and assess the situation objectively. Don't overreact emotionally. Consider criticism to be constructive feedback rather than a personal attack. Recognizing that failures are not the end of the world, and they can aid you in learning to compartmentalize your emotions and pride. Resilience develops with time as new difficulties are confronted.
   - **Benefit:** Leaders who engage in Emotional CrossFit are better equipped to deal with challenges and criticism. This emotional training promotes resilience in the same way that CrossFit improves physical strength. Maintaining objectivity helps you to make sound judgments and lead with confidence. This method promotes a growth mindset and exhibits your adaptability and persistence, much like a CrossFit enthusiast conquering a difficult workout. By cultivating resilience, you may face the difficulties of leadership with serenity, flexibility, and the will to persevere in the face of failures. With your emotional CrossFit practice, you stay psychologically prepared for any leadership challenge, getting stronger with every episode.

2. **Action: "It Is What It Is"**
   - **Technique:** Employ the "It Is What It Is" concept, which supports accepting situations, events, and problems as they

are. Rather than putting yourself and your team through the emotional strain of labeling everything as positive or negative, concentrate on understanding objective facts. Practice perceiving situations from a pragmatic and balanced standpoint.

- **Benefit:** The "It Is What It Is" mindset provides a strong mental tool for you and your team. Accepting things as they are without judgment allows you to maintain emotional stability, decrease stress, and formulate an adaptable culture. This mindset enables you to approach issues with a clear head and make reasoned judgments based on facts rather than emotional emotions. It improves your leadership by exhibiting poise in the face of hardship and encouraging your team to negotiate uncertainty with a calm mind.

3. **Action: Embrace Adversity**
   - **Technique:** Adversity should not be feared and should be viewed as an opportunity for innovation and progress rather than something to be dreaded or avoided. Take on challenges as a chance to generate new ideas and adapt to changing situations.
   - **Benefits:** Acceptance of adversity drives a creative and resilient culture inside your organization and creates a feel-good environment where the team can tackle anything and make a difference. It encourages your team to seek solutions aggressively and to turn setbacks into opportunities for innovation and progress.

4. **Action: Cultivate a Sense of Purpose**
   - **Technique:** Connect your work to a bigger picture of meaning and purpose. Consider how your leadership contributes to your company's goals, helps its stakeholders, and contributes to your own career.

- **Benefits:** Developing a sense of purpose generates motivation and determination, which boosts resilience. Recognizing the importance of your contribution to attaining significant goals motivates you to continue in the face of adversity.

5. **Action: Improve Self-Awareness and Emotion Management**
   - **Technique:** Explore your strengths and weaknesses, guiding principles, and emotional triggers to learn more about yourself. Recognize that, in most interactions, others don't hold power over your feelings; the onus is on you. Embrace your autonomy in deciding how you feel, preventing victimhood to your own emotions. Improve your emotional management by developing acute self-awareness and discipline.
   - **Benefits:** You gain the ability to keep composed under pressure and make educated decisions by realizing your personal control and command of your emotional responses. Acquiring self-awareness not only improves your problem-solving abilities as a leader but also builds credibility and nurtures trust among your team. This trust supports team cohesion and collaborative dynamics. Improved self-awareness not only improves your empathy and communication skills, but it also positions you as a more relatable and resilient leader. Accepting this awareness promotes personal development by allowing you to fine-tune your leadership style and manage problems with patience and adaptability.

6. **Action: Embrace Constructive Feedback**
   - **Technique:** On a regular basis, solicit feedback from coworkers, team members, and mentors. Accept criticism as an opportunity for growth rather than a personal insult.

- **Benefits:** With the help of constructive criticism, you may identify areas for improvement, refine your leadership style, and make sound decisions. It promotes a culture of lifelong learning and demonstrates your commitment to personal improvement.

7. **Action: Active Problem Identification**
   - **Technique:** Look for issues and obstacles inside your group or firm. Finding flaws and inefficiencies early on demonstrates that you are observant and committed to correcting problems as soon as possible.
   - **Benefits:** Actively spotting difficulties allows for early intervention, limiting any negative consequences. It exhibits your ability to solve problems and lead others, earning you respect and trust.

8. **Action: Maintain Work-Life Integration**
   - **Technique:** Strive for work-life balance in order for your personal and professional lives to complement one another. Make time for rest, hobbies, and spending time with loved ones while putting your own health first.
   - **Benefits:** Integrating work and personal life improves resilience by reducing burnout and promoting general well-being. It ensures that you have the energy and emotional power needed to overcome problems and have a happy attitude.

9. **Action: Strengthen Your Social Media Armor**
   - **Technique:** Leaders in the new digital world must avoid taking social media criticism personally. Recognize that the majority of comments are from untrained individuals who may not have a complete understanding of the topics addressed. Reframe negative feedback as opportunities for

progress and constructive criticism rather than personal attacks, bearing in mind that most social media users have good intentions but lack information, and others create drama in order to make themselves feel good and/or collect "likes" and online popularity. Create strategies to keep your cool, such as limiting your social media activity or using moderation tools to filter out problematic content.

- **Benefits:** Thickening your skin as a leader necessitates the development of social media resistance. It allows you to avoid online criticism, maintain neutrality, and focus your energy on worthy topics. By rejecting the impulse to absorb negative social media interactions, you can safeguard your self-confidence and morale, increase your leadership effectiveness, and build a culture of resilience within your organization.

10. Action: Feeding Off Negative Energy

- **Technique:** When confronted with negative comments, criticism, or setbacks, instead of focusing on the negative, channel your energy into something productive. Make an activity or habit for yourself to help you discharge this negative energy. This may be going for a quick walk, exercising, performing a nice act, or allocating dedicated time to work on a meaningful issue.

- **Benefit:** By diverting negative energy into beneficial tasks, you may maintain your resilience and serenity in the face of adversity. It enables you to assess problems objectively by shifting your focus away from unnecessary drama and personalization of criticism. Engaging in a productive endeavor can help you increase your endorphin levels while reducing your stress levels caused by the impacts of increased cortisol levels. This practice improves your ability to lead effectively and inspires your team to approach challenges in a solution-oriented manner.

Chapter Summary

One attribute that regularly emerges as the unsung hero of leadership success is "thick skin." This unique characteristic enables managers to handle the intricacies of their professions with elegance and grace, allowing them to rise above criticism, avoid taking things personally, and assess issues objectively. This chapter addresses the need to manage with resilience and impartiality, as well as redirecting energy away from unnecessary drama and into innovative problem-solving. Recovering from failures, maintaining composure, and understanding that not all criticism is personal insults are all part of the management route to resilience. Objectivity, as a guiding concept, is the ability to assess events rationally and regard problems as solely knowledge-seeking opportunities. Effective managers may guide their teams toward improvements and solutions to challenges. Last but not least, maintaining a positive view in the face of adversity may result in the release of endorphins, which reduces the effects of cortisol, stress, and negative thinking.

CHAPTER 12

ENTHUSIASM IN LEADERSHIP: FROM PASSION TO ACTION

Enthusiasm is a fundamental component; it is the energy that propels groups to success and the passion that sparks innovation. This motivating element is a universal trait that shapes organizational destinies and directs leaders no matter what the profession.

Inspiring Enthusiasm

An outward display of leadership optimism and excitement is a dynamic force that motivates and encourages others to unfounded heights. Genuinely passionate leaders act as role models for their teams, instilling in them the zeal and self-assurance required to overcome hurdles and seize opportunities.

Let us have a look at the fascinating life of Richard Branson, the flamboyant founder of Virgin Group, whose limitless devotion extends far beyond the scope of his commercial activities. Branson's voyage took an especially daring turn when he set out to build Virgin Galactic, the world's first commercial space line.

Branson's charisma and enthusiasm for space travel were not merely abstract ideals; they were tangible forces that sparked the imaginations of millions of people around the world. His charismatic charm and persistent commitment had a way of making dreams come true. Whether he was donning a space suit or speaking to the public about his space exploration plans, Branson's enthusiasm for exploring beyond our planet was contagious.

Richard Branson is more than a CEO; he is a visionary whose power is firmly rooted in his steady desire to venture into uncharted seas. He demonstrates that genuine enthusiasm can serve as a potent energy source for leaders, propelling and guiding their teams toward achieving their goals.

The Confluence of Optimism Action

Instead of being a static emotion, enthusiasm is a dynamic energy that connects optimism and action. It entails having an optimistic view of the future and acting on that positivity. From this perspective, authority acts as a wary guardian, ensuring that this passion is converted into meaningful and advantageous actions rather than becoming a well-meaning distraction.

Consider a situation in which a gung-ho hotel general manager embarks on a revolutionary mission to improve customer experiences. This manager's optimism goes beyond wishful thinking and emerges in a number of ground-breaking initiatives, ranging from personalized welcome gifts to completely immersive cultural experiences for tourists. This leader's enthusiasm functions as a catalyst for positive transformation, boosting the hotel's reputation and patron satisfaction. However, going unfiltered, such passion can create unforeseen consequences, i.e., reduced resources due to reallocation, heightened unbudgeted costs, misalignment with brand standards, etc. Thus, strategic use of such transformative energy is critical.

Leaders who understand the transforming power of enthusiasm recognize that it is an active force that propels teams to remarkable accomplishments. Additionally, their ability to turn optimism into action, inspiring their colleagues to join them on the path to success and pleasure, boosts their influence and their ability to get things done.

The Power of Resilient Enthusiasm

Enthusiasm is more than a fleeting ally in leadership; it is the staunch commitment that remains in the face of adversity. Consider a restaurant manager who, despite a significant decline in sales due to uncontrollable occurrences, never loses enthusiasm. To boost revenue, the management undertakes varied measures to increase income and patronage, including presenting new specials, expanding the menu with new and enticing items, and actively engaging with customers to obtain feedback for the improvement of their dining experience.

Additionally, the manager closely collaborates with the restaurant servers, engaging them in role-playing sessions designed to enhance their up-selling skills. The manager assigns each server a personalized sales target, offering incentives upon successful achievement while fostering a sense of friendly competition within the team. By also underlining the direct link between increased revenue and amplified gratuities, the manager reinforces what is in it for them.

The team seeing this is motivated by this manager's ability to weather the crisis and adapt to the changing scenario. They, in turn, are inspired to change their tactics, offering heightened service and guest satisfaction.

Resiliently passionate leaders recognize that challenges will always arise, but their exhibited belief in their objectives drives and encourages their employees. Their ability to overcome barriers with unrelenting enthusiasm proves that setbacks are simply temporary roadblocks on the route to long-term success.

The Synergy of Personal & Professional Enthusiasm

During my time working in the hotel sector, I witnessed successful leaders routinely combining personal and professional interests. In addition to their professional zeal, these leaders blended their personal hobbies and diversions into their work lives.

Imagine that same general manager, devoted not only to delivering outstanding guest experiences but also is a fervent gourmet. This individual skillfully infuses their love for great culinary experiences into the hotel's atmosphere, resulting in a diverse and exceptional guest journey. Their combined personal and professional passion enhances the hotel's reputation and the experiences of its guests. Incorporating personal and professional excitement promotes creativity, improves the customer experience, and ultimately raises the reputation of excellent leaders in any industry.

Tips & Tricks

1. **Action: Positive Body Language**
   - **Technique:** Maintaining eye contact, smiling, and using expressive motions when appropriate are all characteristics of positive body language. Eliminating closed-off positions, such as crossing your arms, conveys enthusiasm and engagement.
   - **Benefit:** Positive body language enhances communication, makes you more approachable, and builds leadership confidence. This creates a welcoming and respectful demeanor, diminishing any sense of intimidation while facilitating open communication.

2. **Follow-Up Action: Mirror Mastery**
   - **Technique:** Practice mastering positive body language in front of a mirror on a regular basis, a practice also embraced in the hospitality industry, where many restaurants situate mirrors at kitchen egresses to remind staff, especially servers, to maintain a professional demeanor with a warm smile. Take note of your posture, eye contact, gestures, and facial expressions. Make an effort to come across as friendly, confident, and open.

- **Benefit:** You get immediate feedback on your body language when you practice in front of a mirror. You may ensure that you constantly come across as personable and enthusiastic by refining your nonverbal communication skills. This ongoing practice helps you maintain a good and influential presence as a leader by creating an environment where enthusiasm, approachability, and confidence are valued attributes.

3. **Action: Infuse Humor**
   - **Technique:** Bring a sense of lightness and fun to your conversations and meetings. Use humor or amusing anecdotes to relieve stress as necessary.
   - **Benefit:** Humor not only lifts the spirit but also indicates your commitment to creating a pleasant and exciting work environment. It establishes a relationship and makes your leadership style approachable and accessible.

4. **Action: The Power of Playback**
   - **Technique**: Make it a habit of recording yourself to ensure that your speech is always full of energy and enthusiasm and that your body language is approachable and inspirational. While delivering your topic with passion and heart is absolutely essential, this technique offers a precious level of insight. Record your speech or presentation on video and watch and listen to it later. Monitor your gestures, timing, tone, and overall delivery, make appropriate revisions, and record again. Repeat until perfect.
   - **Benefit:** Making a recording of your speech is a powerful self-evaluation tool. It allows you to objectively examine your speech, ensuring that your enthusiasm is conveyed. You can spot times in the recordings when your passion shines through and areas where you might improve. This pattern not only ensures that your speech captivates and holds the

audience's attention but also promotes your position as a passionate and enthusiastic leader.

5. **Action: Harness the Power of Enthusiastic Language**
   - **Technique:** Add impact words to your phrases to energize your writing and speech. To demonstrate your enthusiasm and optimism, use terms such as "exciting," "wonderful," or "opportunity." Avoid using harsh or careless words. "We have some exciting ideas for the project that will certainly push us to success," rather than "We have some other ideas for the project." Your choice of words will inspire and drive your employees, adding energy and enthusiasm to your communication. Powerful words include Electrifying, Thrilling, Remarkable, Exhilarating, Phenomenal, Vibrant, Inspiring, Marvelous, Spectacular, Riveting, Astonishing, and Extraordinary. Search the internet for additional "power" words.
   - **Benefit:** Using positive words creates a more pleasant and stimulating workplace. It instills in your group or peers a sense of possibilities and success.

6. **Action: Express Appreciation**
   - **Technique:** Express thankfulness and admiration when appropriate. Recognize and praise the efforts and successes of others to demonstrate your enthusiasm for teamwork and collaboration.
   - **Benefit:** Through the expression of gratitude, relationships are strengthened, morale is increased, and a culture of passion and appreciation is established. It motivates individuals to continue submitting their finest work.

7. **Action: Genuine Interest**
   - **Technique:** Genuine interest involves actively participating in the current debate, task, or conversation. When you

actually care about something, your excitement shines through. This might include inquisitive questions, a genuine want to understand, and attentive listening.

- **Benefit:** Genuine interest creates a more dynamic and enjoyable atmosphere for both you and the individuals with whom you interact. Your enthusiasm radiates, encouraging others to participate more actively in conversations and activities. As a result, team members' connections develop, and their trust grows, promoting stronger cooperation.

8. **Action: Take Initiative**
   - **Technique:** To demonstrate interest, take the initiative to engage or contribute. Volunteer for chores or projects that are related to your hobbies and interests to demonstrate your devotion and enthusiasm. Additionally, aggressively seek opportunities to propose new ideas or organizational improvements.
   - **Benefit:** Taking the initiative demonstrates that you are a forward-thinking leader. It increases your confidence in your abilities and inspires others to emulate your behaviors, resulting in a more enthusiastic and aggressive team. This proactive mindset promotes not just innovation but also a culture of constant development.

9. **Action: Self-Assess Your Passion**
   - **Technique:** Reflect and ask yourself, "Would my team think I have passion?" This self-evaluation takes into account your degree of excitement and devotion to your work as a leader. Examine your relationships, decision-making, and overall attitude regarding your duties.
   - **Benefit:** Self-evaluation of your passion is a useful introspective practice that may help you judge your dedication and excitement as a leader. Understanding how your team perceives you allows you to find areas for

development and concentrate on improving your enthusiasm. A passionate leader not only inspires their team but also creates a great work atmosphere, promotes innovation, and encourages people to go above and beyond in their positions. This self-awareness may result in more team involvement, improved results, and a more meaningful leadership experience. It's similar to Seneca's writings "Vitae, si bene actae, longa est.," "Life, if well lived, is long enough." This quote suggests that a life filled with purpose and passion is fulfilling, regardless of its length. Regarding leadership, this highlights the importance of quality and depth of one's passion for leading rather than just the quantity of time served.

Chapter Summary

Teams are motivated toward their goals by enthusiasm, which combines optimism with action and persists in the face of adversity. It evolves into dynamic energy that impacts outcomes in a range of businesses rather than just being good on the surface. Genuinely passionate leaders motivate and excite their staff, providing them with the vitality and optimism required to overcome hurdles and grasp possibilities. Because of their persistent excitement, which is not only a fleeting sensation but rather a source of energy, they are able to encourage and lead their teams to uncharted limits. In the context of leadership, enthusiasm is an active force that produces outstanding achievements. It expertly integrates personal and professional interests, improving relationships and increasing corporate reputations. In the dynamic world of leadership, enthusiasm is more than simply a strength; it is the driving force that accelerates progress and transforms vision.

CHAPTER 13

VIGOR UNLEASHED:
A LEADER'S DYNAMIC EDGE

The Essence of Vigor in Leadership

Vigor is emerging as a basic component that propels people and organizations to previously unimagined levels of performance. The two attributes that best represent vigor, which is leadership in action, are a tireless pursuit of growth and an adherence to perfection. Leaders who radiate energy operate as change agents, motivating their workers to work with passion and dedication. Vigor is a vital characteristic that supports ingenuity, resilience, and adaptability in a range of disciplines. In times of turmoil and fast change, strong leaders provide their staff with a sense of direction and purpose.

The Faces of Vigor

Sir Richard Branson exemplifies vigor, which is defined by limitless excitement and an unshakable dedication to advancement. His visionary leadership and enthusiasm have not only defined his illustrious career but have also changed entire sectors ranging from music to space exploration and aviation.

One remarkable example of Branson's vigor is his bold quest to shatter the world's record for flying. In his customary ambitious spirit, Branson engaged in projects such as the Global Challenger and the Virgin Atlantic GlobalFlyer, both of which aimed to circumnavigate the globe nonstop. These daring ventures were more than just flying accomplishments; they reflected Branson's unrelenting pursuit of advancement and determination to push the boundaries of what was deemed achievable. His insatiable passion manifested itself in real activities ranging from taking flight himself to sponsorships that pushed the boundaries of aviation technology.

Serena Williams, an example of steadfast resolve both on and off the tennis court, personifies the concept of vitality, which encompasses both mental and physical dimensions. Williams' pursuit of perfection in her sport, especially after becoming a mother, exemplifies her unbreakable spirit and relentless work ethic. Her leadership extends to addressing societal concerns such as gender equality and racial justice, demonstrating a remarkable degree of mental and physical vitality that spans athletics and leadership, sparking innovation and advancement in each.

Leaders with tremendous zeal, such as Malala Yousafzai, a Pakistani education campaigner and Nobel laureate, can achieve great success. Yousafzai's committed efforts to promote girls' education, despite a near-fatal Taliban attack, have had a profound and far-reaching impact on the world. Her incredible journey from campaigning for education in her own Swat Valley to addressing the United Nations General Assembly demonstrates her steadfast dedication. Yousafzai's passion and unrelenting dedication have permeated not only her own life but have also inspired a global movement for girls' education, driving individuals, governments, and organizations to collaborate toward the common goal of ensuring every girl's right to education. Her narrative demonstrates how zealous leadership can generate change and progress.

The real-world examples of Sir Richard Branson, Serena Williams, and Malala Yousafzai illustrate the revolutionary potential and how vigor accelerates growth in the ever-changing field of leadership, leaving an indelible mark on industries and inspiring future generations.

When Vigor Wanes: The Pitfall of Complacency

Leadership can suffer from a lack of enthusiasm, resulting in stagnation and missed opportunities. Consider Dave, a hypothetical head of a thriving tech startup. Dave quickly established a reputation for his vibrant personality, ground-breaking ideas, and persistent pursuit of greatness. His excitement was palpable, and it propelled the company to greater heights.

However, as the firm grew in size, Dave's leadership approach evolved. He began to rely on the status quo and became complacent within his role. Meetings that were previously vibrant brainstorming sessions became stagnant, and Dave's emotions and directives became predictable.

After previously being inspired by Dave's enthusiasm, team members sensed a shift. They began to yearn for the times when Dave would provide the group with new ideas and inspire them to explore unfamiliar territory. His once-active leadership created a void, and the startup's growth slowed.

In this scenario, Dave's dwindling enthusiasm led to complacency, resulting in the loss of opportunities for creativity and development. The firm, previously known for its innovative ideas, was now unable to compete with competitors that were adaptable and willing to adjust.

Dave's experience teaches the importance of sustaining and promoting energy in leadership. It underlines how even powerful leaders may become complacent if they fail to infuse their jobs with enthusiasm, excitement, and a commitment to growth.

Tips & Tricks

1. **Action: Demonstrating Work Ethic and leading by Example**

- **Technique:** Consistently maintain dedicated work hours, actively participate and collaborate with enthusiasm, pursue continuous learning, demonstrate resilience in facing challenges, manage time effectively, foster open communication, uphold ethical standards, prioritize health and wellness, engage in community involvement, and showcase a commitment to personal and professional growth.
- **Benefit:** Leading by example and demonstrating a strong work ethic has the added benefit of instilling that same work ethic in the rest of the team. When leaders are willing to invest the time and effort required to achieve, their teams are inspired to do the same.

2. **Action: Vigorous Goal Setting**
    - **Technique:** Setting intense and inspiring objectives for yourself and your team is an example of aggressive goal setting. These goals should push the limits of what is possible, generate motivation, and challenge the status quo.
    - **Benefit:** Strong goal setting yields a culture of continuous development and establishes a high standard for achievement. It takes the firm to new heights by pushing individuals to move outside of their comfort zones and innovate.

3. **Action: Assemble Cross-Generational Collaboration**
    - **Technique:** Encourage your workforce's intergenerational collaboration and knowledge sharing. Recognize and cherish the many perspectives and life experiences that each generation brings.
    - **Benefit:** Encouraging intergenerational collaboration improves the overall vitality of your workforce. It creates a dynamic and creative work environment by combining the

passion and new ideas of younger team members with the expertise and experience of more experienced ones.

4. **Action: Pursue Passion Projects**
   - **Technique:** Encourage team members to work on initiatives or projects that align with their passions and interests, even if they go above and beyond their normal responsibilities. Provide them with the necessary resources and guidance to pursue these passion projects, and allow them to share their progress and insights with the team.
   - **Benefit:** Pursuing passion projects ignites individual enthusiasm and creativity. It stimulates internal drive, resulting in more innovative ideas and a greater sense of purpose among team members.

5. **Action: Unyielding Energy**
   - **Technique:** Portraying unyielding energy is like a never-ending source of inspiration and resolve. It is the persistent commitment to maintaining high levels of enthusiasm and tenacity. Vigorous leaders understand the importance of staying motivated and actively keeping their energy up in order to progress both themselves and their people.
   - **Benefit:** Unrelenting energy benefits the entire business by setting a lively and robust tone. When leaders consistently display boundless excitement, it inspires individuals to approach work with zeal, developing a can-do attitude and group desire to overcome problems and achieve goals.

6. **Action: Upbeat Attitude**
   - **Technique:** An optimistic attitude is a mode of thinking that continuously sees the best in situations and sees setbacks as chances to grow. Vigorous leaders understand the significant impact that keeping positive, especially under difficult situations, can have on staff morale and motivation.

- **Benefit:** An optimistic mindset has the added benefit of spreading positivity across the organization. Leaders who are consistently optimistic and resilient inspire their followers to do the same. As a result, the organization's ability to adapt, innovate, and flourish despite adversity is enhanced.

7. **Action: Resilience & Resolve**
    - **Technique:** Demonstrate resilience and determination by facing challenges and setbacks without losing enthusiasm or dedication. Maintain unwavering focus and determination, viewing setbacks as opportunities for growth and learning while anchoring your goals and values in the process.
    - **Benefit:** The benefits of resilience and dedication include the promotion of an enduring culture inside the company. Leaders who demonstrate resilient commitment in the face of adversity provide a good example for their employees to follow. This resilient and determined culture ensures that setbacks are viewed as opportunities for growth and innovation, leading to even greater success.

8. **Action: Perpetual Motion of Progress**
    - **Technique:** To keep development going forward, a forward-thinking mentality must be maintained. Vigorous leaders continually seek opportunities for growth and advancement. They continuously urge their employees to consider other options since they are dissatisfied with the existing scenario.
    - **Benefit:** The benefit of constant advancement is that it keeps the organization adaptable and inventive. When leaders pursue development persistently, they build a culture in which change is welcomed rather than feared. Because of its innovative culture, the company is able to keep one step ahead of the competition and prosper in difficult conditions.

9. **Action: Inspire Through Unflagging Determination**
   - **Technique:** As a leader, you should avoid overtly confessing to being weary or whining about working additional hours or days. Instead, focus on becoming a continual example of dedication, perseverance, and fortitude. Your actions and attitude should motivate your team by exhibiting your commitment to the goal and desire to put in the necessary effort to make it a success.
   - **Benefit:** A strong work ethic sends a powerful message to your employees. It inspires people to endure in the face of adversity and hard hours, as well as to push their personal boundaries. Leading with enthusiasm and excitement stimulates an environment of endurance and devotion, eventually encouraging your team to greater accomplishments and success.

10. **Action: Enthusiastic Engagement**
    - **Technique:** What is meant by enthusiastic engagement is participating in activities and conversations with real excitement and energy. Leaders must be able to identify when and where they need to infuse a heightened level of energy to optimize their team's performance.
    - **Benefit:** Participation that is enthusiastic has the advantage of creating a positive and energetic climate inside the group or organization. Leaders who are consistently enthusiastic about their jobs inspire their employees to approach their work with the same eagerness and dedication. This leads to increased productivity, creativity, and overall job happiness.

11. **Action: Looking Good, Feeling Good**
    - **Technique:** Vitality needs a strong physical base. Leaders who prioritize their physical well-being understand how it influences their vigor, mental clarity, and overall vitality. They actively devote time to activities that promote physical

fitness, such as exercising, eating a nutritious diet, and getting adequate sleep. Additionally, leaders downplay tiredness, being sick, or feeling stressed out.

- **Benefit:** Physical health benefits leaders by increasing their capacity to maintain high levels of vitality and focus. When managers prioritize their physical health, their staff observe and learn. This boosts individuals' productivity while also establishing a positive business culture based on a wellness culture.

Chapter Summary

Vigor is emerging as a basic component that propels people and organizations to previously unimagined levels of performance. The two attributes that best represent vigor, which is leadership in action, are a tireless pursuit of growth and a tireless adherence to perfection. Vigorous leaders effect good change by motivating their followers with energy, passion, and determination, paving the road for remarkable achievement. This chapter investigates the different aspects of leadership vigor and its revolutionary potential to encourage innovation, resilience, and adaptation across a variety of sectors. Leaders who are equipped with enthusiasm motivate their people and convert hurdles into opportunities in times of uncertainty and fast change. Vigor propels growth in the fast-paced world of leadership, leaving an indelible mark on sectors and inspiring future generations.

CHAPTER 14

THE POWER OF APPROACHABILITY:
THE BRIDGE BUILDER

Approachability is the route to meaningful encounters and open communication. It enables leaders to enhance unity, confidence, and inclusion among their teams. Team members may readily communicate their ideas, concerns, and critiques to approachable leaders in both formal and informal settings. This flowing interaction breaks down barriers and encourages impromptu idea exchange.

Trust thrives in a nurturing environment. When team members regard leaders as approachable and transparent, trust grows. Trust is essential for collaboration because it promotes cooperation, risk-taking, and devotion to common goals. Employees are motivated to go above and beyond in a trustworthy workplace because they know their efforts are valued.

Great leaders in the modern workplace have the capacity to be accessible. Rather than a one-size-fits-all technique, it entails an attitude of openness, empathy, and active involvement. Approachable executives build a culture of cooperation, trust, and inclusion, which contributes to the organization's success.

Being Approachable: Nelson Mandela's Mastery

Approachability is essential for effective leadership, and few people exhibit this trait more clearly than Nelson Mandela. Mandela not only demonstrated exceptional approachability throughout his extraordinary life, but he also made it the centerpiece of his work. Because of his ability to connect meaningfully with a wide spectrum of audiences, he is considered a leader par excellence.

The pillars of Nelson Mandela's technique to approachability are genuineness, empathy, and a remarkable confidence in the power of human connection. His career began as an activist and leader in the anti-apartheid campaign, where he spoke about social justice and equality with people from all walks of life. Mandela was notable for his ability to listen to and comprehend his fellow activists and citizens actively. He understood the underlying emotions and experiences as well as the words themselves. He could ask observant questions that frequently yielded meaningful replies. In its safe and judgment-free environment, people felt comfortable communicating their most fundamental feelings and wishes.

From Activism to Leadership Legacy

Nelson Mandela's approachability extended beyond political lobbying. During his presidency in South Africa, he actively pursued discussions and peace, particularly in the face of a deeply divided nation. His leadership demonstrated how cordiality can bridge even the widest chasm, providing a source of inspiration not just for his country but also for the whole global community. Nelson Mandela's life exemplifies the transforming power of approachability, as he was instrumental in encouraging conversation, peace, and reconciliation inside a severely divided South Africa. His capacity to create true personal relationships not only characterized his enduring legacy but also had a significant and long-lasting influence on society. His example serves as an anguished reminder that accessibility may inspire empathy and establish transnational ties.

Being Happy

No one ever wants to work with a miserable boss. Leaders who are sincerely joyful and cheery have a huge influence on their surroundings, the workplace as a whole, and organizational culture. They want to be friendly, but they also want to transmit joy and build a positive community. When team members witness their leaders' genuine enthusiasm, it becomes contagious. This excitement not only boosts morale but also encourages creativity and problem-solving abilities. A CEO who is personable and joyful develops a culture in which team members are motivated, encouraged, and appreciated.

Conversely, it is damaging when a leader is regularly unhappy at work or, worse, never happy. Such an atmosphere may result in demotivated team members, higher stress levels, and a toxic work environment. A lack of approachability and cheerfulness in a leader may stifle creativity, hinder cooperation, and weaken trust. In these circumstances, leaders must be aware of the consequences of their conduct and take proactive steps to remedy it because their attitude and disposition have a substantial impact on the firm's culture and success.

Tips & Tricks

1. **Action: First Impressions: Make them Count**
    - **Technique:** Begin each engagement with a genuine, welcoming smile, eye contact, and a firm handshake. Engage in active listening by asking open-ended questions to stimulate discussion. Demonstrate genuine attention to the other person's replies.
    - **Benefit:** Making a good first impression is important because it changes how others view you and their attitudes toward you. According to psychological research, first impressions are established quickly, within milliseconds after an interaction. They have a long-term influence on people's

trust, credibility, and desire to connect with you. Beginning conversations with a welcoming smile, eye contact, and a strong handshake projects warmth, confidence, and sincerity, which improves people's perceptions of you. Active listening and genuine interest in other people's comments build rapport and connection, making them more likely to open up and create a constructive relationship with you. Remember that you seldom have a second chance to make a first impression, so make the most of it.

2. **Action: Smile**
   - **Technique:** When initiating a conversation with someone for the first time, make sure to offer a warm, genuine smile that engages your eyes and facial muscles. Allow your eyes to crinkle slightly at the corners to create a Duchenne smile that conveys authenticity. Maintain a comfortable and welcoming expression, avoiding overdoing it while maintaining sincerity.
   - **Benefit:** When you smile, your body undergoes a series of uplifting chemical responses. As a consequence, endorphins, which naturally boost mood and relieve pain, are released, while stress hormones like cortisol are reduced. When someone smiles, dopamine, a neurotransmitter related to pleasure and reward, is also produced. It may also result in decreased blood pressure, enhanced immune system efficiency, and even relaxation of the facial muscles over time.

     Furthermore, when you smile in front of someone, their brains react. When their mirror neurons detect your facial expressions, they activate and generate a sympathetic response. When people see your genuine smile, endorphins are generated in them as well, elevating their mood and promoting a nicer social atmosphere. Smiles have the power to boost not just your own mood but also the relationships and well-being of people around you.

3. **Action: Maintain Open Body Language**
   - **Technique:** Adopt a relaxed posture, refraining from crossing your arms and ensuring your gestures are non-threatening.
   - **Benefit:** Open body language is essential for efficient communication. According to research, these indicators assist in developing trust and fostering communication. Maintaining open body language projects warmth and honesty, making others feel at ease approaching you. It communicates a lack of defensiveness as well as a readiness to engage in a meaningful discourse. Those are drawn to people who use open body language because it indicates a friendly disposition, which promotes greater communication and collaboration.

4. **Action: Maintain Eye Contact**
   - **Technique:** To use this approach effectively, make sure your eye contact is pleasant, courteous, and balanced, avoiding both extremely intense glances and excessive avoidance. While the other person is speaking, look them in the eyes, acknowledging their words and emotions.
   - **Benefit:** Maintaining eye contact with the other person throughout a discussion is a powerful nonverbal sign of approachability. Making eye contact shows the other person that you're totally engaged in the conversation, interested in what they're saying, and eager to connect on a personal level. Avoid making overly direct or scary eye contact; instead, achieve a natural and comfortable balance.

   Eye contact is necessary for approachability and efficient communication. It builds rapport, conveys respect, and improves communication standards. When others perceive you to be truly interested in them and attentive to their presence, they are more likely to feel valued and at ease.

Maintaining good eye contact may assist you in developing strong relationships and engaging talks.

5. **Action: "Man In The Mirror"**
   - **Technique:** Consider your normal resting facial expression when you're not actively emoting. Examine your look in the mirror or consider how you appear when you are not speaking to someone, or you think no one is looking.
   - **Benefit:** It's critical to understand how your resting facial expression influences how others see you. It makes you aware of the first impression you make on others, whether it is one of approachability, friendliness, neutrality, or something altogether else. As the popular song "Man in the Mirror" reminds us, sometimes the person gazing back at you is the person who can help you change. By being aware of this perspective, you may make appropriate modifications to ensure that your nonverbal communication reflects your intended image and supports pleasant relationships. To get a more objective assessment, ask a close friend or family member what they honestly think of your relaxed facial expression.

6. **Action: Practice Active Listening**
   - **Technique:** When you actively listen to someone's views and opinions, you show that you value them. Maintain eye contact with the speaker to demonstrate that you are paying attention. You can demonstrate real interest in what they are saying by nodding and utilizing voice signals such as "I understand" or "Tell me more."
   - **Benefit:** Active listening strengthens relationships and connections. It promotes open communication and shows respect for other people's points of view. People enjoy being heard and are more likely to interact with someone who is interested in what they have to say.

7. **Action: Express Gratitude for Issue Reporting**
   - **Technique:** Make it a habit to say "Thank you" swiftly and honestly anytime someone brings an issue or worry to your attention. "Thank you for bringing this to my attention," you may remark. Make sure your tone and body language convey that you actually appreciate their willingness to communicate their concerns, and avoid coming across as if this is just another problem to add to your already overburdened plate. When addressing a concern to your supervisor, it's critical to remember how you want to be treated and to act appropriately.
   - **Benefit:** When someone raises a problem, expressing appreciation demonstrates that you appreciate their initiative and honesty. It encourages a positive feedback cycle in which individuals value their contributions, even if those efforts include pointing out flaws. You may encourage individuals with difficulties to come forward by creating an environment in which they feel heard and valued. This generates an open atmosphere and enhances future development. This develops open communication, promotes trust, and leads to improved problem-solving and organizational development.

8. **Action: Use Welcoming Physical Gestures**
   - **Technique:** A strong yet welcoming handshake, eye contact, and a smile are conventional ways to greet someone and develop rapport. Handshakes, fist bumps, and friendly waves are all acceptable welcoming gestures. As many subordinates may be hesitant to greet a superior, you should always initiate the greeting; this is also beneficial in making a good first impression.
   - **Benefit:** Forthcoming and traditional greetings establish a sense of inclusion and harmony. They help to establish rapport quickly and mitigate any first impression issues. Such activities indicate your warmth and desire to connect.

9. **Action: Initiate Conversations**
   - **Technique:** Taking the initiative to begin conversations with strangers or to introduce oneself demonstrates that you are receptive to social engagement.
   - **Benefit:** Starting conversations indicates your kindness and willingness to interact with others. It assists in breaking the ice and putting others at ease when approaching you. This proactive approach can help to develop the groundwork for meaningful interactions and can lead to fruitful commercial and personal ties.

10. **Action: Respect Personal Space & Boundaries**
    - **Technique:** Respect personal boundaries and avoid invading another person's individual space, but also acknowledge that different cultures have various methods of greeting, and being conscious of these distinctions is crucial, especially while working in varied workplaces.
    - **Benefit:** Respecting people's space and cultural differences shows that you are interested in their well-being. When people feel comfortable and appreciated in the setting you create, they are more inclined to engage with you.

11. **Action: Offer Encouragement & Support**
    - **Technique:** Actively listen, provide support, and motivate. Understand viewpoints, exhibit empathy, aid in problem-solving, and recognize accomplishments. Demonstrate trust in team members' abilities. Develop open communication and collaboration by being receptive to direction and cooperation.
    - **Benefit:** Support and encouragement help to build trust and positive connections. It encourages people to contact you when they need help or direction, building relationships and collaborations that benefit both sides. People are more

inclined to approach someone whom they believe to be encouraging.

Chapter Summary

Approachability is the road map to open communication and the formation of deep bonds. Approachability is a feature that links numerous professions and allows leaders to create inclusion, cooperation, and trust among their staff. They provide an environment in which team members may express their ideas, thoughts, and concerns without fear of reprisal. Being personable is critical. Approachable leaders demonstrate respect to every customer and staff member, regardless of status or background. They adhere to the highest etiquette standards and value each individual's dignity. By implementing these practices into your relationships, no matter the industry, you can project a kind and accessible aura, encouraging others to approach you and engage in meaningful conversations. Being accessible is a leadership method that enhances connections and bridges gaps across sectors. It's also important to remember that as a leader, genuine enjoyment of your work environment and life in general can greatly boost your approachability factor. Your excitement and pleasure can create a pleasant climate within your team that encourages trust and open communication.

CHAPTER 15

LEADERSHIP IN THE AGE OF EMPATHY

Empathy, at its core, is a fundamental concept in interpersonal relationships, acting as a connecting force between people. It includes the ability to understand and share the feelings, thoughts, and perspectives of others, which, when used effectively, results in strong, collaborative, and enriched human connections. However, empathy, like any other tool, has limitations. This chapter delves into the nuances of when and how to practice empathy while remaining effective as a leader, providing a thorough understanding of this critical concept.

The Importance of Understanding

Empathic leaders have an incredible ability to understand the thoughts and feelings of those they lead. They recognize that true understanding is required for effective leadership.

Consider Nelson Mandela, the famous anti-apartheid campaigner and former South African president mentioned in the chapter on Approachability. Mandela's tremendous empathy for his country's varied communities was a defining feature of his journey from prisoner to president. He was aware of the pain, worries, and hopes that were important to his people's survival.

Mandela's compassionate leadership opened the way for South Africa's peace and unity, demonstrating that empathy entails more than just pity for people; it also entails understanding their experiences. Empathic

157

leaders encourage true connections and trust among their employees, advancing a culture in which everyone's perspective is valued and heard.

Empathy in Action: Acknowledgment & Validation

When appropriate, recognize and affirm the other person's feelings to assure them that what they are feeling is authentic and valid. "It's extremely normal to feel this way in such a circumstance," you may say.

When the following empathetic techniques and strategies are applied, the ideals of strategic leadership excellence are personified. They advocate for acceptance, inclusion, support, and positive change.

- ❖ **Sincere Assistance:** Empathy is typically followed by action. "Is there anything I can do to help?" or "There are resources available" are wonderful ways to convey support. If they consent to your help, be prepared to follow through.
- ❖ **Empathetic Silence:** The most sympathetic reply is to say nothing at times. Allow the individual to express themselves without fear of being judged or put under pressure to provide solutions.
- ❖ **Empathetic Non-Verbal Cues:** Maintain eye contact to convey attention and involvement. So that the speaker feels heard and acknowledged, your facial expressions should be friendly and empathetic. Nodding indicates active listening.
- ❖ **Inquisitive Exploration:** To urge the speaker to express themselves more completely, use open-ended questions such as "How do you feel about that?" or "Can you share more about your experience?" These questions can elicit more powerful emotional responses.

Where Empathy Meets Professionalism

Approachability requires a combination of empathy and sensitivity, which goes beyond basic accessibility. Strong leaders recognize the need for work-life balance, highlighting the importance of setting boundaries and standards. This comprehensive approach entails not just displaying sympathy and giving support but also, if necessary, making unpleasant decisions.

Consider the case of a leader who is approachable but disciplined. This leader understands the need for workplace boundaries while also providing empathy and aid to team members experiencing personal issues. This skillful blending of empathy and professionalism develops the leader's interaction with team members and promotes an environment of accountability and shared responsibility.

In today's workplace, leaders must strike a balance between developing a strong work ethic and sympathetic conduct. Leaders must demonstrate empathy and support for younger generations in the workplace, but they must not pamper them. An effective leader is responsible for teaching, inspiring, and keeping their team members accountable by instilling the ideas of hard work and learning via personal devotion and perseverance. Leaders should instill in their team members the importance of working hard, accepting challenges, and refusing to perceive themselves as victims when asked to put in the effort required to achieve. This method ensures that the team remains committed, resilient, and driven, allowing the organization to flourish in the long run.

Knowing When to Let Go

Leaders, despite their best efforts and compassion, occasionally discover that certain people are not a good match for their team or organization. It is critical to avoid wasting time and money on retraining someone who may be a hopeless case. If an individual's discontent with their current position has a detrimental influence on the working environment as a whole, leaders should, through the proper means, encourage them to search for a position where they may be happier and more productive. This technique ensures that one person's discontent does not have an impact on the health and morale of the entire team.

Approachable leaders use their influence wisely, understanding when to elicit empathy and when to make decisions that maintain a healthy workplace atmosphere. Their power is bolstered not just by their ability to connect with their teams but also by their dedication to the overall success and peace of the workplace.

Empathetic Leadership: Timing Matters

A discerning leader, talented in understanding empathetic behaviors and strategic timing, comprehends the versatile application of these principles, both in interpersonal interactions and personal endeavors. This nuanced insight empowers exceptional leaders to optimize various leadership dimensions, including delegation, task distribution, critical feedback, brainstorming sessions, interviews, negotiations, and other pivotal aspects.

To maximize productivity, astute executives strategically schedule favor requests, creative brainstorming, and innovative initiatives at opportune times. Recognizing that timing affects many aspects of human behavior, including tolerance, agreeability, resourcefulness, creativity, adaptability, and time commitment, tactical leaders deliberately schedule and launch activities and meetings accordingly. For example, they understand that Mondays are dedicated to catching up after the weekend, Fridays require focus on completing the week's work, and post-lunch periods see a decrease in energy and tolerance levels. Leaders also recognize that Tuesday and Wednesday mornings, before lunch, are ideal for tapping into people's increased receptivity and creative capacities. Simultaneously, clever leaders conduct negotiation activities shortly after lunch, leveraging the post-meal lull when individuals are more predisposed to agreement and less willing to put up a fight. Recognizing the impact of this behavior on themselves, leaders may opt for an early or light lunch to ensure peak negotiation efficacy. These strategic techniques align with the natural cognitive patterns of the workweek, increasing the total impact of empathetic leadership practices.

Employing empathy entails not only understanding individuals but also appreciating the larger context of their circumstances, which leads to enhanced effective leadership practices.

Tips & Tricks

1. **Action: Active Listening & Understanding**
   - **Technique:** Active involvement in one-on-one sessions with team members is required for active listening and deep comprehension practice. This entails not just listening to what people have to say but also delving deeper to comprehend their points of view, emotions, and issues. It necessitates paying attention to the subtle nuances and nonverbal cues that serve to construct a more complete picture of their experiences.
   - **Benefit:** When you utilize active listening at this fundamental level, it indicates your commitment to learning the intricacies of your team members' experiences. By addressing their unspoken sentiments and concerns, you can adopt a trusting environment in which open communication thrives and better relationships and collaboration ensue.

2. **Action: Feedback & Improvement Dialogues**
   - **Technique:** Empathy is critical in feedback and improvement discussions because it transforms constructive criticism into an opportunity for change. In addition to the mere transmission of feedback, it entails a sincere attempt to grasp the emotional components of the recipient's experience. It means addressing areas that want development while also giving actual support and practical solutions. During a team meeting, Sachiko, the team's leader, mentioned that Alex had been struggling with recent tasks. Sachiko adopted an accommodating position throughout

their one-on-one feedback session. Before inquiring about the areas that required improvement, she questioned Alex about his prior experiences and how he felt about the issues he was facing. She actively listened to his concerns and conveyed her admiration for his feelings. Sachiko then assisted Alex in identifying specific areas where he could benefit from support and provided ideas on how to overcome those difficulties. She made it a point to express her confidence in his talents and to emphasize that the feedback was designed to help him succeed.

- **Benefit:** Team members' resilience is enhanced, and their personal growth is improved by introducing empathy into feedback sessions. It ensures that feedback is not seen as criticism but rather as a tool of continuous progress, encouraging a culture of growth.

3. **Action: Setting Empathetic Expectations**
   - **Technique:** Building sympathetic workplace norms needs more than merely declaring how vital empathy is. It entails setting clear standards that safeguard professionalism while encouraging team members' collaboration and understanding. These standards are predicated on acts of empathy, resulting in a workplace where empathy is more than simply a theoretical concept but a daily practice.
   - **Benefit:** Setting such norms contributes to the creation of a workplace in which compassion and productivity are the norm. It forms a tranquil environment in which empathy naturally flows into daily interactions, enhancing interpersonal relationships and a sense of belonging.

4. **Action: Recognizing & Celebrating Milestones**
   - **Technique:** When leaders take the time to consistently identify and celebrate their team members' personal and professional accomplishments, empathy emerges in the

context of recognizing and marking milestones. It entails going above and beyond official appreciation to show genuine interest in each person's unique experiences and accomplishments.

- **Benefit:** This caring approach to recognition demonstrates how much you actually respect your team's efforts and experiences. It communicates a deep understanding of their particular journeys, improving team morale and instilling a sense of appreciation and unity.

5. **Action: Balancing Compassion & Accountability**
   - **Technique:** Offering help, comprehension, and empathy while holding team members answerable for their performance and actions are all aspects of establishing a balance between compassion and accountability in leadership. It demonstrates the ability to comprehend the problems that individuals may face while maintaining clear goals and standards.
   - **Benefit:** This mix of compassion and accountability keeps empathy from being misconstrued as indulgence. It develops a culture in which team members understand the need to maintain standards, accept responsibility for their actions, and strive for excellence, ultimately increasing productivity and individual growth.

6. **Action: Navigating Tears and Emotions**
   - **Technique:** Maintaining a professional and sympathetic demeanor during counseling sessions is crucial, even when dealing with employees' tears or emotional outbursts. It's important to understand that emotional responses, including crying, can be defensive mechanisms that might not be appropriate in a professional setting. Should these defense tactics arise, encourage the individual to take a moment to gather themselves rather than let these feelings disrupt the

conversation. Suggest a brief break so they can regain emotional control and rejoin the conversation in a cool, collected manner.

- **Benefit:** This method of addressing emotional toughness in counseling makes sure that the office environment is productive and professional. By gaining understanding it allows the manager to distinguish between real-life, intensely emotional circumstances—like the death of a loved one—and defensive measures like crying or sob stories., so they may act accordingly. During the latter, by allowing employees a moment to collect themselves, you can keep your team's attention on the problem at hand and collaborate to find solutions. By fostering a culture of emotional intelligence, empathy, and professionalism, this technique encourages more beneficial and productive interactions at work.

7. **Action: Encouraging Continuous Learning & Growth**
   - **Technique:** To support continual learning and progress, it is vital to construct a work culture that emphasizes ongoing personal development. It is comprised of actively encouraging and empowering team members to take responsibility for their learning process, as well as aiding them in their efforts to enhance their knowledge and talents.
   - **Benefit:** Such an environment is completely compatible with empathetic leadership since it allows individuals to evaluate, grasp, and improve themselves. It contributes to the development of a competent and content workforce, which supports both individual and organizational progress.

8. **Action: Prudent Decision-Making for Team Dynamics**
   - **Technique:** In the context of team dynamics, judgment is required while examining the team's makeup and interactions. It entails detecting situations in which an employee may not be a suitable match for the team dynamics

and, rather than employing punitive measures, entice them to pursue jobs more suited to their strengths and personality.

- **Benefit:** Prudent decision-making develops a pleasant and successful work environment by putting the team's overall well-being and morale first. It advances a sense of community and collaboration while allowing people to thrive in roles where they can contribute most effectively.

Chapter Summary

Empathy serves as a guidepost for relationships, a link between individuals, and a means to understanding. Empathy is a strong tool that impacts relationships, inspires collaboration, and improves the human experience, among other things. Empathic leaders have an incredible ability to understand the thoughts and feelings of those they lead. They recognize that true understanding is required for effective leadership. Empathy requires acknowledging and respecting others' feelings, offering genuine support, being sympathetically calm, and using nonverbal cues and exploratory investigation to foster understanding. Furthermore, in the ever-changing world of leadership, approachability goes beyond basic accessibility; it is dependent on the fusion of empathy and sensitivity. Approachable leaders recognize the need for work-life balance, highlighting the importance of setting boundaries and standards. This comprehensive approach entails not just displaying sympathy and giving support but also, if necessary, making unpleasant decisions. Empathy is a strategic leadership tool that promotes a culture of comprehension, inclusion, support, and positive development in order to sustain the objectives of strategic leadership excellence.

CHAPTER 16

INSPIRE TO ASPIRE:
ELEVATING EXCELLENCE

Leadership inspiration acts as the spark that ignites an organization's culture of excellence. A successful leader's primary goal is to help those around them achieve success on both personal and professional levels. It is through tangible achievements that true inspiration finds its foundation and spreads its influence. This invigorating force propels individuals not just to surpass their own expectations but also to pursue loftier objectives while nurturing a culture of continual development. This transformative quality serves as a common thread across all industries, inspiring managers to bring out the best in their team members.

Gandhi's Inspirational Legacy

Motivating leaders inspire their staff with a clear purpose and goal, similar to Mahatma Gandhi's commitment to obtaining India's freedom peacefully. Mahatma Gandhi's unrelenting drive and ability to unite millions from varied backgrounds in pursuit of a shared goal are timeless examples of transcending personal interests and promoting unity in the field of leadership. His nonviolent resistance-based struggle for India's peaceful independence stands as a remarkable example of inclusion and the need to bridge societal differences. Gandhi's leadership also emphasizes personal sacrifice, as seen by his incarceration, fasting, and persistent commitment to his ideas, which inspires others to make similar sacrifices for their causes.

Furthermore, his embodiment of simplicity and humility, living a humble life and prioritizing values above material wealth, connects with people, prompting them to reassess their priorities and values. His activism for social justice, addressing disparities, and combating prejudice inspires others to fight for the rights of the vulnerable.

Leaders who embody Gandhi's moral authority lead with integrity, sincerity, and consistency, instilling trust and belief in their teams. They, like Gandhi, use the transformative power of inspiration to effect meaningful and positive change in a variety of fields.

The "Why" Technique

When striving to inspire others, outstanding leaders employ the "why" method. By starting with the core reason, "the cause," the belief or event that motivates their efforts, leaders can create a meaningful connection that goes beyond the typical "what" and "how." Consider Alex, a manager in the medical equipment industry, who addresses his workforce not with a laundry list of tasks or goals (the "what" and "how") but rather by emphasizing the company's underlying "why." Alex states that the company's aim is to save lives and improve healthcare outcomes by innovating, producing, and marketing medical equipment. This collective confidence in the larger objective energizes the team, focusing their efforts in the same direction. People are inspired and motivated when they recognize the profound importance of their actions and how they align with the organization's core values. Consequently, exceptional leaders, such as Alex, can utilize the "why" approach to structure and motivate individuals, facilitating remarkable accomplishments in their industry.

The Motivator of Extraordinary Efforts

In sports, inspirational leaders are frequently found among coaches, who have the unique ability to encourage athletes to go above and beyond and achieve greatness, similar to how a soccer coach motivates his team of underdogs with the inspirational objective of winning the championship. These coaches understand that inspiration acts as a catalyst for people to overcome their apparent limitations.

A highly motivated coach inspires his players to exceed their own limits of play but also to support one another and persevere even in the face of adversity. This inspirational leadership strengthens the team's performance, allowing them to reach their championship goals. It emphasizes the idea that true inspiration ignites a fire within people to achieve extraordinary feats; it is more than just motivation.

The Champion of Continuous Growth

Inspiring leaders promote both the continual growth of their teams and their own personal development. They motivate their coworkers to accept change as a method of reaching greatness and hammer into them the belief that there is always room for development. Elon Musk, the innovative CEO of firms such as SpaceX and Tesla, is a perfect example of this type of leader.

Musk's uncompromising belief in the practicality of space travel and sustainable energy has inspired a slew of engineers and inventors. His outstanding leadership has not only pushed the boundaries of technology but has also motivated others to work in these cutting-edge areas. Musk's ideas and activities reflect his notion that motivating people needs leading by example, conquering challenges, and viewing failure as an opportunity to grow.

Elon Musk's inspiring leadership extends beyond his innovative ideas. He instills in his teams a feeling of purpose and urgency, underlining the crucial relevance of their job for the future of mankind. Musk's devotion to Mars colonization, for example, acts as a powerful incentive for his teams, driving them to innovate and tackle challenging issues. His commitment to sustainable energy solutions pushes his workforce to confront environmental concerns head-on.

Musk's management style also includes cultivating a culture of continuous learning. He encourages his teams to learn new skills, whether they are in engineering, renewable energy, or space exploration. Musk's investment in employee development benefits not only his organizations but also individuals, allowing them to grow and expand their knowledge, which aligns with his belief in continuous self-improvement.

Collective Achievement

Motivating leaders inspire their people to go above and beyond what they are capable of or willing to do. They represent the belief that the accomplishments of the team as a whole are considerably more meaningful and enduring than any individual accolades and that genuine success is measured by the team's overall performance. Their primary goal is to develop a culture of collaboration and joint accomplishment.

Inspiring leaders are the sparks that ignite the flames of collective brilliance inside their teams. They motivate employees to exceed their own expectations, achieve more difficult goals, and build a culture of continuous growth. They inspire people across sectors to bring forth the best in themselves and their teammates.

To properly implement this method, check in with your team on a regular basis to acknowledge and praise even their small accomplishments. This can take numerous forms, including direct comments, team-wide acknowledgments, or small rewards. It is critical to make team members feel valued and appreciated for their efforts, no matter how minor they may appear.

Maintaining a Positive Attitude: The Resilience of Optimism

Positivity spreads swiftly. Maintain a cheerful attitude, especially in the face of adversity. Encourage your employees to see challenges as opportunities for growth and learning. You inspire your team to confront obstacles with tenacity and ingenuity by maintaining a positive attitude and perseverance, which leads to more success. Your untiring optimism inspires your team to trust in their talents by serving as a beacon of hope while they traverse turbulent waters.

Tips & Tricks

1. **Action: Understanding "What's in It for Them"**
   - **Technique:** Talk to your team in detail and empathically to understand their innermost motives, future goals, and core beliefs. Encourage team members to express themselves freely by asking open-ended questions and listening carefully to their responses. Pay close attention to their body language, emotional expressions, and any nonverbal cues. Examine their previous accomplishments and moments that brought them pride or a sense of achievement.
   - **Benefit:** This detailed process is critical for tailoring your approach to motivating someone to achieve. Paying attention and deeply engaging in meaningful discussions can help you understand the individual's unique motivators and sources of inspiration. With this knowledge, you may tell a tale that relates their personal aspirations to the bigger team or corporate goals. This close relationship demonstrates your genuine concern for their development and well-being, and it builds a strong sense of purpose and commitment. As a result, they are more likely to pursue their ascension to greatness with unwavering commitment and joy.

2. **Action: Harnessing the Power of the Inner Spark**
   - **Technique:** Concentrate on producing intrinsic motivation by aligning activities and initiatives to employees' passions and interests while increasing your understanding of their motivations and beliefs. Encourage them to find meaning in their job by connecting it to their personal beliefs.
   - **Benefit:** Employees who are encouraged to pursue their intrinsic drive have a great feeling of fulfillment and purpose. When individuals have a sense of purpose in their job, they are more likely to go above and beyond and remain committed to achieving the organization's goals. This technique ensures that their internal drive remains a source of inspiration, increasing their commitment to and enthusiasm for the pursuit of greatness.

3. **Action: Crafting the "Why" Message**
   - **Technique:** Crafting the "Why" message entails transforming your organization's or initiative's core values, motivations, or goals into a compelling narrative. Discovering the underlying purpose of your actions necessitates careful consideration. Once identified, articulate this "Why" message in a way that deeply connects with your intended audience, whether they are your employees, customers, or stakeholders. Use storytelling, impactful language, and genuine enthusiasm to convey the "Why" in a memorable and emotionally engaging way.
   - **Benefit:** By concentrating on building and articulating the "Why," your leadership will be able to inspire and engage people powerfully. By building a shared sense of purpose and conviction, this strategy nurtures stronger ties and commitment. People who understand and identify with the "Why" are more motivated, dedicated, and committed to your cause, which leads to higher production, new ideas, and long-term success for your company or cause.

4. **Action: Encourage Intrapreneurship**
   - **Technique:** To encourage intrapreneurship within your organization, create an innovative culture, allocate necessary resources, recognize and reward innovative contributions, give employees the freedom to experiment and explore ideas, create collaborative spaces, provide mentorship and feedback mechanisms, implement project tracking, and actively communicate and celebrate intrapreneurs' successes to inspire and motivate others.
   - **Benefit:** Through intrapreneurship, employees are given the power to own their ideas and turn them into viable businesses. It instills in employees a sense of responsibility, inventiveness, and ownership, motivating them to contribute actively to the company's growth and success.

5. **Action: Empower & Delegate**
   - **Technique:** Giving employees considerable responsibilities and decision-making ability inside their workplace is a critical component of empowering them. Delegation allows team members to accept responsibility for their work, which encourages them to be proactive problem solvers and decision-makers.
   - **Benefit:** Employees who believe they are respected and driven have more power. They get a sense of freedom and accountability, which increases job satisfaction and pride in their work. This technique also encourages team leadership growth and offers you more time to focus on strategic duties.

6. **Action: Lead by Example**
   - **Technique:** Your team looks to you as a leader to set a good example. When you consistently demonstrate devotion, professionalism, and ethical behavior, your workforce has a clear example to follow. Your commitment to the company's

ideals and work culture sets a good example for your employees to follow.

- **Benefit:** Strong leadership advances mutual trust and respect. Because they can witness your honesty and passion, your team is more likely to trust your leadership. This technique builds a culture of accountability in which everyone strives to meet the same high standards.

7. **Action: Encourage Innovation & Creativity**
   - **Technique:** Encourage employees to think creatively and to share their innovative ideas. Create a culture that supports innovation and continuous improvement. Provide team members with locations or chances for brainstorming so that they may collaborate on new ideas and solutions.
   - **Benefit:** Encouragement of creativity and innovation results in new ideas and techniques, which supports organizational growth and flexibility. Employee engagement and work satisfaction are boosted since it allows them to offer their unique perspectives.

8. **Action: Recognize & Reward Achievements**
   - **Technique:** Employee efforts and successes must be recognized and rewarded in a timely and particular manner. Celebrating successes, no matter how big or little, in public encourages the qualities and contributions you value.
   - **Benefit:** Rewards and recognition boost morale, motivation, and work satisfaction. They show employees genuine appreciation, making them feel valued and treasured. Over time, this method increases employee loyalty, productivity, and engagement.

9. **Action: Create Inspiring Special Moments for Recognition**
   - **Technique:** Take the initiative as a leader to create and carry out special events or occasions to recognize and acknowledge exceptional people in your team or organization. This might include throwing a celebration or simply paying them a personal visit at work. Make sure the appreciation moment is well-planned and designed to make the recipient feel truly valued and appreciated.
   - **Benefit:** This inspires the person and others around them by generating an unforgettable moment of appreciation. It sends a clear message that hard work and dedication are respected and rewarded. This gesture lifts morale, promotes an appreciation-based culture, and motivates team members to give their all. Furthermore, it creates a sense of belonging and strengthens team bonds, which increases dedication and productivity. Be mindful that, in some cases, honoring both the person and the entire team may be acceptable in order to encourage inclusion and cohesiveness.

10. **Action: Provide Growth Opportunities**
    - **Technique:** Access to training, mentoring, and possibilities for professional progression are all part of providing growth opportunities. Employees can expand their knowledge and capabilities by being given the opportunity to learn new things and develop new skills.
    - **Benefit:** Giving your staff advancement opportunities demonstrates your commitment to their professional development. It creates loyalty and retention by exhibiting your dedication to their professional growth. As employees learn new skills and knowledge, they become more valuable assets to the organization.

11. Action: Kevlar Coating

- **Technique:** Imagine yourself with a Kevlar coating, the embodiment of tenacity and strength, when guiding your team through difficult times. Stay calm and confident, prioritize concise and transparent communication to build trust, maintain a stable and consistent environment, define a clear path forward, demonstrate personal resilience, encourage innovation, and celebrate small victories and progress to inspire and guide your team effectively.

- **Benefit:** Leadership in the face of adversity demonstrates your strength and leadership confidence. Collectively, these behaviors improve your team's ability to face problems with tenacity and unity. Employees feel more secure as a result of improved trust and certainty. It also enhances team cohesion and resilience, allowing the organization to navigate difficult situations more successfully.

12. Action: Flexibility & Work-Life Balance

- **Technique:** Recognizing and addressing people's different needs and well-being is critical to developing flexibility and work-life balance. It is critical to provide flexibility through a variety of channels, such as vacation time, paid time off (PTO), sick days, and flex days, to enable individuals to manage their personal and professional lives efficiently, establishing a harmonious balance.

- **Benefit:** Supporting work-life balance improves employees' overall well-being and mental health. Burnout, stress, and absenteeism all go down. Employees are more likely to be productive, engaged, and committed to the firm when they sense their needs are being met and that they can maintain a healthy work-life balance.

Chapter Summary

By directing team members with a strong sense of purpose, inspirational leaders encourage their colleagues to achieve tough goals and overcome personal restrictions. They promote continual progress and perceive difficulties as opportunities to improve. They also place a great value on collective performance, emphasizing the need for collaboration. The chapter also discusses effective leadership techniques such as establishing a positive example, empowering others, and delegating, as well as strategies for promoting work-life balance, encouraging innovation, and recognizing and rewarding accomplishment. These techniques are meant to foster a supportive work environment that promotes development and organizational success.

CHAPTER 17

LEADING WITH LAUGHTER:
HOW HUMOR ENHANCES EFFECTIVENESS

My boss said, "I want you to treat this company like it's your own." So, I started looking for a buyer...

Unknown

Whereas it is usual to carry a lot of weight on one's shoulders, there is a hidden gem: the power of laughter. This chapter discusses the importance of having a sense of humor and how to utilize it as a tool for effective leadership.

The Gift of Laughter

Consider a leader who has the uncanny ability to make everyone in the room laugh or smile at the appropriate time. This boss possesses a very special trait. Humor is more than just telling jokes; it is about creating an atmosphere of lightheartedness and comfort for others. It's not always essential to laugh aloud; sometimes, just making someone smile is a gift in and of itself. A simple grin can alleviate stress, lessen tension, and generate an enthusiastic atmosphere. As we'll see in this chapter, the power of a grin, a witty statement, or an amusing event can have enormous benefits for leaders and their teams.

Southwest Airlines co-founder Herb Kelleher was well-known for his remarkable use of humor to establish a healthy and entertaining workplace atmosphere. He went beyond words to incorporate humor into his leadership style with amusing remarks and colorful pranks. During workplace events, for example, he would dress up in costumes, participate in amusing plays, and even perform magic tricks, all with the goal of lightening the mood and encouraging employee camaraderie.

Kelleher's approach to humor was instrumental in not just permitting but also fostering a lighter culture at work. His leadership demonstrated that humor can be a potent weapon for breaking down social barriers inside an organization. It had the effect of breaking down hierarchical distinctions, making it easier for employees, regardless of their positions or roles, to connect with one another. Kelleher's ability to merge humor with leadership demonstrated that work does not have to be unduly serious and that a pleasant and healthy work atmosphere can lead to higher employee satisfaction and productivity, ultimately contributing to Southwest Airlines' success and unique culture.

Funny Business: A Guide to Perspective

Leaders with a sense of humor not only use laughter to their advantage, but they also recognize the importance of maintaining perspective. They recognize that many of the challenges and setbacks that appear significant at first are frequently minor annoyances when viewed in context. This awareness enables them to more effectively allocate their attention and resources, focusing on what truly matters in the grand scheme of things.

Consider this scenario: a leader suffers a setback, such as a project delay or a minor financial glitch. Rather than being absorbed by frustration or despair, the leader cuts the tension with a light-hearted anecdote, keeping their eye on the bigger perspective. The leader understands that setbacks are an inescapable part of leadership, and, more importantly, they understand the need to manage them productively.

In essence, leaders who incorporate humor into their leadership style not only utilize laughing as a tool but also employ perspective to better handle problems. They teach their colleagues that keeping a sense of humor and perspective can help minimize the impact of obstacles and disappointments, ultimately developing a resilient and flexible work culture.

Laughter Is The Best Medicine

Incorporating humor into leadership has been scientifically proven to relieve stress. When leaders find humor in the face of hardship, it has the extraordinary potential to release tension and enhance mental clarity. Humor, according to science, causes the production of endorphins, the body's natural feel-good chemicals that not only improve mood but also work as natural stress relievers. Leaders who use humor in their approach are frequently better suited to dealing with high-stress situations.

For instance, consider a manager who is dealing with an unanticipated crisis. Rather than giving in to the pressure, this leader injects humor into a team meeting, utilizing humor to lighten the mood. This method provides more than a temporary reprieve; it has a physiological influence. Laughter causes the release of endorphins, which not only helps to reduce emotional tension but also increases creative problem-solving abilities, as stress may sometimes block rational thinking. As a result, humor may be seen as a crucial weapon in a leader's toolbox, acting as a scientifically validated stress-reduction strategy that not only generates a happy work atmosphere but also improves the team's ability to deal with obstacles efficiently.

Tips & Tricks

1. **Action: Ice Breaker Humor**
   - **Technique:** To use humor as an icebreaker effectively, you must first grasp your audience's tastes and sensibility. It is critical to customize your humor to their preferences, ensuring that it is contextually appropriate and relevant to the circumstance at hand. You may create a more engaging and collaborative environment by using humor that develops camaraderie among team members. However, maintaining the meeting's objectives requires striking a balance between professionalism and enjoyment. Use humor that creates a lasting impression to ensure that participants remember the meeting or presentation with a sense of positivity and camaraderie.
   - **Benefits:** By reducing stress and promoting a positive mood, humor promotes a more comfortable and open environment for cooperation and debate.

2. **Action: Storytelling with Humor**
   - **Technique:** Craft narratives infused with humor to effectively convey your message, drawing inspiration from various sources, such as personal accounts or recent events. For instance, recount a memorable team-building event where a particularly over-enthusiastic colleague attempted a trust fall exercise with hilarious results, which serves as an engaging illustration of the significance of effective team communication and trust-building.
   - **Benefits:** Such amusing stories captivate and retain your audience's attention, boosting your storytelling talents and making your message more remembered and accessible. They generate a nice and fun environment that enhances the ties between your team members by establishing a culture of camaraderie and shared experiences.

3. **Action: Self-Deprecating Humor**

   - **Technique:** Make light of yourself or your team in a humble and non-offensive manner. To utilize self-deprecating humor effectively, it is important to achieve the proper balance. The goal is to light-heartedly make fun of yourself or your group in such a manner that others laugh without feeling uneasy. Avoid being excessively harsh or self-critical in your humor.
   - **Benefits:** You become more relatable and likable by making fun of yourself. It can defuse tense situations and demonstrate your humility.

4. **Action: Office Humor & Inside Jokes**

   - **Technique:** Create and share lighthearted workplace humor and inside jokes with your team. Make certain that the humor is inclusive and not offensive or disparaging to anybody. The goal is to utilize humor to build the team rather than alienate anyone.
   - **Benefits:** Office levity encourages a sense of community, strengthens team bonds, and contributes to the development of a pleasant office culture, which boosts morale and productivity.

5. **Action: Harnessing Surprise Humor**

   - **Technique:** Add unexpected humor to meetings, emails, or other interactions when appropriate to leverage the element of surprise. During a particularly long and complex team meeting, for example, you may inject a lighthearted joke or an amusing tale. You might also send your coworkers a witty and surprising email that employs humor in a way that is suitable for the task or scenario at hand.
   - **Benefits:** Unexpected and spontaneous humor may have a huge impact on the workplace. It keeps everyone engaged

and attentive even during the most basic and dull activities or meetings. When humor is used in the workplace, it adds energy and excitement, increasing job satisfaction and establishing a pleasant environment.

    i.   Surprise humor benefits more than just mood; it may boost workplace chemistry, communication, and overall efficiency. It encourages collaboration and fun among colleagues, which helps to deepen their bonds. Furthermore, it demonstrates that you are a likable leader who understands the human side of business, encouraging a more relaxed and open working climate in which creativity may flourish.

    ii.   To add surprise and spontaneity into your leadership style, you don't have to turn every contact into a comedy routine. Instead, it's about recognizing situations in which a well-timed, amusing touch may substantially change the environment, bringing enjoyment, connection, and revitalized life to the workplace.

6. Action: Positive Feedback with Humor

- **Technique:** Celebrate successes by delivering supportive criticism or witty praise. "You're like a ninja of efficiency— quick, silent, and always one step ahead of the game," you may remark to someone on your team who has excellent time management skills.

- **Benefits:** Humorizing positive feedback not only acknowledges and rewards successes, but it also adds a beautiful and amusing touch to the workplace. This method encourages your staff to continue their exceptional job by encouraging good actions. As a consequence, the team members feel valued and inspired to keep up their multitasking circus performance. This culture of cheerful recognition and positivity is promoted.

7. **Action: Problem-Solving with Playfulness**
   - **Technique:** Bring a lighthearted approach to problem-solving sessions, when appropriate, to encourage brainstorming and creative thinking. For example, you may start a team meeting to discuss a difficult project impediment by presenting a silly hypothetical circumstance. This playful approach may spark creative thinking and help your team think beyond the box.
   - **Benefits:** Playful problem-solving reduces the likelihood of failure, enhances creativity, and yields innovative solutions. If you incorporate some levity into your problem-solving process, your team will become more adaptable and imaginative. This strategy creates a culture of experimentation and discovery, which may lead to game-changing breakthroughs and a more enthusiastic workforce.

8. **Action: Distinguishing Wit from Humor**
   - **Technique:** Spend some time figuring out the difference between wit and humor. Wit is defined as the capacity to communicate intellect and sharpness in a quick, witty, and often subtle manner. Humor, on the other hand, encompasses a broader range of emotions and can range from lighthearted enjoyment to loud laughter. Pay attention to how these features are employed in different circumstances, whether in debates, presentations, or written content.
   - **Benefits:** Knowing the distinction between wit and humor allows you to adapt your communication approach to different situations and target groups. Knowing when to utilize wit or humor will improve your communication and leadership skills. It promotes stronger interpersonal

connections, better partnerships, and the establishment of a productive workplace. Knowing whether to utilize wit and humor depends on the circumstance and the desired outcome, so being aware of this provides you with a beneficial communication tool.

Chapter Summary

This chapter explores the usually underappreciated capacity of humor as a weapon. It emphasizes the importance of developing a sense of humor and how to use it to build a supportive and resilient workplace culture. Humorous leaders put people at ease and lighten the mood. Humor provides leaders with a unique perspective that allows them to stay focused on what matters most and manage setbacks gracefully. It functions as a stress-reduction tool, allowing leaders to deal with high-stress circumstances with more clarity. Humor in leadership advances teamwork, humanizes the workplace, and creates a happier and more productive workplace. This chapter also discusses techniques like icebreaker humor, storytelling with humor, self-deprecating humor, office humor & inside jokes, harnessing surprise humor, positive feedback with humor, problem-solving with playfulness, and distinguishing wit from humor.

Section III
Navigating Leadership Challenges

Welcome to Section III: Navigating Leadership Challenges, where we will expertly navigate the difficult terrain of leadership. We examine the characteristics that can help you meet leadership challenges head-on. From acquiring perspective, progressing from manager to leader, changing your team's thoughts and futures, and guiding a group to greatness via team building. We'll also look at time management as well as leadership in motion, popularly known as the art of managing by walking around. So, as we confront these leadership difficulties, let us open the door to the knowledge required for success.

CHAPTER 18

FROM MICRO TO MACRO:
THE DUALITY OF A GREAT LEADER'S FOCUS

Learning to understand a focal viewpoint is similar to learning to walk a tightrope. It entails an ironic challenge: avoiding caring about little details on the one hand and paying close attention to detail when it actually counts on the other. This chapter examines how critical it is to establish this balance, as well as the enormous impact it may have on effective leadership.

The Weight of Leadership

Consider a leader who meticulously scrutinizes every aspect, from the arrangement of office décor to the font size utilized in a presentation. While paying attention to detail has its benefits, going too far can result in micromanagement and an unpleasant work atmosphere. Such executives risk inadvertently restricting innovation, impeding development, discouraging their employees, and losing sight of the larger picture goals.

A leader, on the other hand, who consistently rejects small matters as trivial may unintentionally develop a culture in which crucial details are disregarded. This might lead to errors, inefficiencies, and missed opportunities. Finding the elusive middle ground becomes critical to effective leadership.

A Real-Life Example: Steve Jobs & Apple

Consider the legendary Apple Inc. co-founder Steve Jobs. Jobs was a leader who paid close attention to detail where it was most important. He was well-known for his formidable commitment to design quality and user experience. When it came to Apple product design, he was obsessed with the smallest details, such as the colors used in the casing of a MacBook and the shape of an iPhone's sides.

However, Jobs did not micromanage every aspect of how Apple conducted business. He was aware that there were some tasks he should delegate to his team. He was known for having high standards for product design, but he delegated more general aspects of engineering, production, and marketing to others.

This harmony allowed Apple to innovate and construct ground-breaking products while maintaining a work environment that valued quality and innovation. Steve Jobs exemplified the concept of perspective; he knew when to focus on the specifics that comprised Apple's brand and when to delegate responsibility for the bigger picture. His legacy demonstrates the importance of honing this complex leadership skill.

A Captain Can't Steer the Ship If He's Working in the Engine Room

The idea that "A Captain Can't Steer the Ship If He's Working in the Engine Room" underpins the calibration of positions in leadership. Leaders utilize calibration as a compass to identify the importance of various facts in various situations. Effective decision-makers use a mental compass to direct their actions and determine where to direct their limited time, energy, and attention.

Leaders who have mastered the concept of perspective understand the need for finely calibrated systems. They recognize the need to pay meticulous attention to every detail while making critical decisions or in times of crisis. In these conditions, they accept their responsibilities in the engine room and endeavor to ensure that every aspect of the ship's functioning runs well.

However, these seasoned leaders recognize that when the repercussions are minor, they may gracefully abandon perfectionism in normal actions or circumstances. Instead of concentrating on minutiae, they steer the ship towards its bigger goals. The captain's role is an example of this calibrating concept, which enables leaders to thrive at both navigating turbulent waters and charting a steady path toward success.

Effective Delegation

Developing perspective also includes the ability to assign tasks that need close attention to detail. Leaders who can identify team members with the requisite expertise and ability for certain tasks ensure that important details are addressed without overburdening themselves or their team members.

Consider a busy marketing agency manager who works with a team that includes a skilled proofreader. The manager correctly allocates this task to the talented team members, allowing them to shine in their area of specialty rather than manually inspecting each page for minute typographical problems. This not only decreases the manager's burden but also allows team members more autonomy to take ownership of their allocated jobs.

Attention to Detail: The Power of the Red Pen

Meticulous attention to detail is pivotal in leadership, serving as the bedrock of precision, quality, and overall success in various daily operational aspects. Whether applied to project management, decision-making, or team development, this commitment to thorough scrutiny ensures that no critical components go unnoticed. Precision doesn't just boost accuracy but also reduces errors and bolsters accountability, fostering professionalism and trust among stakeholders. Leaders who prioritize this level of detail are better equipped to spot opportunities, preempt obstacles, and make strategic decisions. Essentially, it forms the essence of exceptional leadership, nurturing continuous growth and equipping leaders to navigate the intricacies of business. This systematic focus is akin to the red-pen-wielding teachers of our past, transforming our ordinary homework into a masterclass of fine-tuned precision. Think of it as "fine-tuning" as the path to success, much like those papers adorned with red ink made us better students. Over time, it helps us all assess our performance more effectively, ensuring that we consistently excel in leadership.

Tips & Tricks

1. **Action: "Trust," a Four-Letter Word**
   - **Technique:** Recognize that when it comes to paying strict attention to detail, the phrase "trust" is usually a four-letter word. Establishing robust checks and balances within your team or organization is your responsibility as a leader to ensure proper adherence to processes and job completion. Use quality control methods, extensive review procedures, and clear accountability structures to decrease mistakes and maintain accuracy across all activities. Accept the notion that confidence should be earned via consistent performance and verification rather than taken for granted.
   - **Benefit:** You build a culture of accountability and quality by emphasizing the dangers of assuming that attention to detail has been thoroughly followed. The usage of checks and balances develops faith in your team's reliability and correctness. This proactive technique ensures that standards are followed on a regular basis while also eliminating mistakes. Your commitment to accuracy and quality is a

characteristic of your leadership, which eventually boosts your group's and company's credibility.

2. **Action: Prioritization of Key Objectives**
   - **Technique:** Concentrate on identifying and ranking your company's most critical goals and tasks. Differentiate between what is truly important and what can be outsourced or set aside by assigning varied degrees of priority to different initiatives and circumstances.
   - **Benefit:** Setting priorities allows you to spend your time and resources more efficiently while concentrating your attention on the things that will have the greatest impact. Focusing on the big picture and strategic goals allows you to maintain your organization's vision clearly while decreasing stress caused by little issues.

3. **Action: Delegation & Empowerment**
   - **Technique:** You may empower your team members by assigning appropriate roles and responsibilities. Trust your employees to handle regular or small concerns, and give them the authority to make decisions within the scope of their responsibilities.
   - **Benefit:** In addition to decreasing your workload, delegating promotes team participation and progress. Team members gain skills and confidence, and you have more time to focus on making strategic decisions. This method reduces the stress caused by minor issues and micromanagement.

4. **Action: Flexibility & Adaptability**
   - **Technique:** Accept adaptability and flexibility as vital leadership characteristics. Accept that not everything will go as planned, and be prepared to alter your route as needed. Dealing with unanticipated difficulties necessitates having a solution-focused mindset.

193

- **Benefit:** If you are adaptable, you can readily deal with little disturbances and adjustments. It increases team resilience and reduces stress by encouraging a proactive reaction to minor setbacks.

5. **Action: Time Management & Boundaries**
   - **Technique:** Set clear limits and employ effective time management practices. Set aside focused, undisturbed time for strategic thinking while creating time blocks for dealing with emails, minor problems, and administrative tasks.
   - **Benefit:** Time management and limits prevent little, everyday concerns from interfering with your essential responsibilities. They allow you to maintain control of your schedule and reduce stress caused by frequent breaks and diversions.

6. **Action: Insisting on Proper Written Communications**
   - **Technique:** Establish a high-quality expectation for written communications inside your business. In all written contact, including emails, reports, memos, and papers, emphasize the importance of professionalism, clarity, language, and spelling. Encourage the usage of style guidelines and templates to maintain uniformity.
   - **Benefit:** By requiring properly written communications, you establish a high standard for attention to detail across your business. Team members' commitment to quality is obvious when they consistently submit clear, error-free written materials. This strategy also reduces the chance of misunderstandings and miscommunications caused by poorly written material. Furthermore, it promotes an accuracy and thoroughness culture, increasing the probability that other areas of the work, such as project execution, quality control, and documentation, will be handled with the same level of care. Overall, prioritizing outstanding written

communications helps to adopt a culture of detail-oriented practice that pervades all aspects of your organization's activities, increasing overall effectiveness and professionalism.

7. **Action: Quality Control Measures**
   - **Technique:** Set up dependable quality control methods that include routine evaluations and checks at various stages of a project or activity. Assign certain team members the responsibility of quality control.
   - **Benefit:** Quality control processes aid in finding and correcting errors or oversights early in the process, preventing them from escalating into more significant issues. This proactive approach improves the overall quality of deliveries and client satisfaction.

8. **Action: Regular Audits, Inspections, & Reviews with Employee Involvement**
   - **Technique:** Include your team in the process as soon as possible to improve the efficiency of routine audits, inspections, and reviews. Allow team members to conduct inspections while you observe and provide guidance. In order to encourage greater understanding, ask them to point out any defects, and if they do, ask them what the criteria are for those problems to ensure they get rectified properly.
   - **Benefits:** This technique adds an extra layer of staff involvement and growth to the auditing process. It empowers your team to be in control of quality assurance and meticulousness. By involving team members, you further a feeling of accountability and obligation. Team members also have a better understanding of expectations and standards, which improves performance and makes workers more focused. This approach not only identifies and corrects

defects in detail but also develops a culture of continuous development, which leads to higher-quality outputs.

9. **Action: Automation & Technology**
   - **Technique:** Use technology and automation to make operations more efficient and to reduce the possibility of human error. Implement software or systems that aid in data verification, consistency checks, and error detection.
   - **Benefit:** Automation reduces the need for manual inspections, lowering the possibility of human mistakes. It boosts job productivity, precision, and consistency, thereby raising the level of attention to detail throughout your organization.

10. **Action: Recognition & Rewards**
    - **Technique:** Create an incentive and recognition system that recognizes individuals or groups for their exceptional attention to detail. Celebrate successes and highlight instances when detailed planning paid off.
    - **Benefit:** The positive feedback loop produced by recognition and awards will drive your workers to prioritize attention to detail consistently. This strategy promotes the importance of the frequent use of diligence in a culture.

11. **Action: Preemptive Checklists**
    - **Technique:** Make extensive checklists to ensure you complete all critical phases for assignments or projects. When making a checklist, begin by breaking the work down into more manageable sub-tasks. Include any deadlines, duties, dependencies, and contingencies. Set priority for your tasks to help you stay on track, and check off completed tasks as you go.

- **Benefit:** Checklists promote efficiency and dependability by reducing the potential of omission or error by carefully guiding you through activities. They provide comfort that crucial details have been addressed, and their well-organized structure encourages a deliberate approach to difficult tasks.

12. **Action: Proofreading Tools**
    - **Technique:** To detect errors in written documents, utilize grammar and spell-checking software such as Grammarly or the built-in software in Microsoft Word. Once completed, run the work through the program to identify and correct any grammatical, spelling, punctuation, and style errors.
    - **Benefit:** Proofreading software improves the quality of written papers by detecting and correcting errors, ensuring that your messages are accurate, clear, and polished. In order to save time and effort, they automate the proofreading process.

13. **Action: Templates**
    - **Technique:** Use templates for papers, presentations, and spreadsheets to maintain consistency in structure and organization. Templates give a rigorous framework, which reduces the possibility of formatting errors. Maintain the existing framework while updating templates to match your specific needs.
    - **Benefit:** Using templates expedites document development while also ensuring a professional appearance. They reduce the possibility of mistakes caused by manual formatting while also saving time. Using templates allows you to focus on the content rather than the formatting components.

14. Action: Revision Time

- **Technique:** Set aside a specific amount of time after completing a task for revisions and proofreading. Do not rush through the review process. Throughout the review period, examine your work meticulously, paying particular attention to language, formatting, and content correctness.

- **Benefit:** Dedicated review time allows for laborious improvement, minimizing the likelihood of errors and ensuring that the final output meets high standards. It helps you to maintain consistency and professionalism in your work.

15. Action: Triple-Check Numbers

- **Technique:** When working with financial data or statistics, double-check numerical figures and equations several times to avoid costly mistakes. Create a rigorous number verification approach that involves computations, cross-referencing, and data entry.

- **Benefit:** It is critical to triple-check your figures to avoid financial blunders and miscalculations. It ensures that data-driven judgments are based on accurate information that has been thoroughly verified, minimizing financial risks and improving decision-making.

Chapter Summary

This chapter explores the delicate balance that exceptional leaders must achieve between paying precise attention to detail and knowing when to step back and look at the broader picture. The weight of leadership can lead to two extremes: micromanagement when detail is important and a disregard for elements when it matters too little. The chapter emphasizes the significance of achieving this balanced calibration for effective leadership. Real-life examples, such as Steve Jobs' leadership style, show the significance of perspective mastery. The notion that "A Captain

Can't Steer the Ship If He's Working in the Engine Room" emphasizes the importance of well-balanced leadership focus. Leaders must utilize a mental compass to direct their efforts and allocate their time and attention wisely in order to succeed. Leaders can successfully traverse this paradox by embracing growth, defining clear priorities, effective delegating, adaptability, and a range of strategic tactics. The chapter also discusses techniques encompassing trust and attention to detail, prioritization of key objectives, delegation and empowerment, flexibility and adaptability, time management and boundaries, properly written communications, quality control measures, and regular audits, inspections, and reviews with employee involvement.

CHAPTER 19

THE POWER OF DELEGATION:
BE A LEADER, NOT A MANAGER

Mastering delegation is like leading a symphony. It necessitates agility, precision, and a good understanding of when to seize the reins and when to pass them over to others. This chapter examines delegation as a multipurpose tool that frees up a leader's time while also empowering teams and developing leadership within an organization.

Time Management: Streamlining Priorities

Smart leaders recognize that time, like everything else in life, is a limited resource that has a big impact on their overall performance. In the intricate dance of managing various tasks and duties, delegation emerges as a basic time management method. It provides leaders with the invaluable chance to focus their resources on more critical strategic objectives and activities, enhancing their effectiveness and productivity.

Skill Development: Nurturing Growth

Task delegation not only saves workload but also enhances skill development. Leaders who delegate provide their team members with the opportunity to grow and learn. Talent development produces more skilled and adaptive employees, which eventually improves the organization's overall capabilities. Consider the well-known filmmaker Steven Spielberg. He is well-known for cultivating the potential of emerging filmmakers through mentorship and delegation, in addition to his remarkable directing abilities. By delegating authority and providing advice, he has assisted these individuals in honing their filmmaking skills and developing them into highly accomplished experts in the entertainment industry. Over the years, he has empowered and guided many others, allowing them to hone their filmmaking skills and flourish in the entertainment industry. J.J. Abrams is a tribute to Spielberg's talent and leadership, having directed multiple renowned film franchises such as "Star Trek," "Mission: Impossible," and "Star Wars." Not only has Spielberg's effective delegating and mentorship enhanced the film business, but it has also demonstrated how empowering others can lead to tremendous growth and success.

Finding Equilibrium

Leadership is a marathon, not a sprint. Effective delegation is the key to achieving a harmonious work-life balance. Leaders can keep their energy levels up and avoid burnout by delegating tasks to their teams. This balance not only promotes personal well-being but also creates a positive working environment, setting a good example for the team.

Increased Productivity: Accelerating Progress

Delegation expedites growth by distributing tasks to the proper individuals. This not only benefits the firm but also helps executives focus on higher-level thinking and decision-making, enhancing productivity. Furthermore, this extra mental capacity may be leveraged to stimulate collaborative creativity.

Leaders build a dynamic atmosphere in which team members are given the flexibility to own their tasks as they delegate. Leaders can freely explore new ideas, techniques, and possibilities because they are no longer bound by specific duties. This increased potential for innovation and invention may result in the development of unique solutions and perspectives on current issues.

Consider Kay, a bright entrepreneur, and her tech business. Kay is able to dedicate more time and mental energy to researching cutting-edge technology, industry trends, and growth plans by delegating day-to-day operational tasks to talented team members. This proactive approach to delegation not only benefits the business but also generates an inventive culture in which team members are encouraged to offer their unique thoughts and suggestions.

Delegating in this manner creates a fertile atmosphere for innovation to flourish, hastening the process and propelling the company to new heights of productivity and success.

Scalability: Jeff Bezos' Blueprint for Expanding Leadership Impact

As leadership expectations may not be fully realized as businesses evolve, delegation is the key to scalability. To grasp this concept, look no further than Jeff Bezos' pioneering journey—the man responsible for inventing Amazon.

Not only an online bookshop, but Bezos' business adventure also aimed to build a digital retail empire that would alter commerce. However, as Amazon expanded its reach beyond books, it became evident that no single individual could control every facet of such a vast enterprise.

Bezos' ability to expand was revealed when he efficiently divided responsibilities within Amazon. He awarded crucial responsibilities to brilliant individuals while promoting a culture of innovation and adaptation throughout the organization. Through this delegation, Bezos was able to expand the influence of his leadership, and Amazon was able to move with unparalleled agility through the problems of e-commerce, cloud computing, and various ventures.

Jeff Bezos' biography serves as a stark reminder of how important scalability is to great leadership. His strategic delegation boosted his impact and illustrated that, despite wide aims and continuously changing circumstances, leaders who embrace scalability can tap into their teams' capabilities to seize opportunities and overcome challenging challenges.

Tips & Tricks

1. **Action: Delegate Authority, Not Just Tasks**
   - **Technique:** When power is removed from accountability, failure is unavoidable. Giving team members the ability to decide on things relevant to the duties they have been assigned is an example of effective delegation. Allow them to make their own decisions without continuously seeking your approval.
   - **Benefit:** Delegation of authority produces more successful operations by encouraging team members to accept responsibility for their jobs. This expedites decision-making and nurtures accountability and ownership among your team members.

2. **Action: Hire Experts & Get Out of Their Way**
   - **Technique:** It is not your responsibility as a leader to be an expert in every discipline but rather to surround yourself with knowledgeable Subject Matter Experts (SMEs) who excel in their particular domains. It is your obligation to find these specialists, empower them, ensure they have the appropriate resources, instill the goals, and allow them to take the lead in their areas of expertise. This method entails actively searching out top SMEs and entrusting them with duties and projects that are relevant to their competence. Check on as necessary to ensure direction, support and guidance.

- **Benefit:** By surrounding yourself with experienced and competent SMEs and providing them with autonomy in their disciplines, you may build a highly successful and efficient team. This strategy leads to higher productivity, better problem-solving, and inventive solutions. It also develops a culture of cooperation and mutual respect in which each team member's abilities are fully used. Furthermore, as a leader, this strategy allows you to focus on your personal skills and strategic goals while ensuring that your firm benefits from the aggregate knowledge and abilities of your team.

3. **Action: Match Tasks to Team Members' Passions**
   - **Technique:** Identify your team members' passions and interests, as well as their strengths and weaknesses. When assigning tasks, align responsibilities with team members' genuine interest in the work.
   - **Benefit:** Delegating work based on passion results in greater job satisfaction, engagement, and innovation. Team members who are enthusiastic about their work tend to put in more effort and pay more attention to detail, resulting in remarkable results. It also raises morale since team members value the opportunity to work on issues that actually interest them.

4. **Action: Rotate Delegation Responsibilities**
   - **Technique:** Encourage team members, regardless of seniority, to take turns leading projects or delegating duties. This rotating distribution of delegation assignments exposes team members to different aspects of leadership and gives a sense of ownership in the group's overall performance.
   - **Benefit:** Rotating delegation tasks provides considerable leadership experience to a broader spectrum of team members. It promotes a common leadership culture and

helps individuals thrive. Furthermore, it prevents over-reliance on a single leader by splitting the workload and encouraging cooperation.

5. **Action: Delegation Feedback Loops**
   - **Technique:** Implement feedback loops for delegation. Conduct debriefings in which both the team members who received the delegation and the leader who delegated give input before, during, and after the completion of a work or project. Discuss what is working, what may be improved, and any lessons learned.
   - **Benefit:** Delegating feedback loops promote continuing learning and evolution of the delegation process itself. They allow the leaders to guide individuals back on the right path if needed, strengthening their delegation skills, and allowing them to assign duties more successfully in the future. Team members also have a better understanding of their own performance, which will enable them to grow and evolve with their roles.

6. **Action: Task Decomposition**
   - **Technique:** When allocating hard or diversified assignments, break them down into smaller, more manageable ones. Each subtask, as well as its due date and dependencies, should be defined in great detail.
   - **Benefit:** Task decomposition enhances the organization and clarity of allocated work, reducing the likelihood of misunderstandings or missed deadlines. Furthermore, because each subtask can be tracked independently, progress may be tracked more efficiently. Finally, it contributes to more efficient task completion and better outcomes.

7. **Action: Encourage Peer-to-Peer Delegation**
   - **Technique:** Encourage peer-to-peer delegation within your organization or group. Encourage team members to distribute tasks to their coworkers based on their availability or area of expertise. This technique promotes peer collaboration and responsibility sharing.
   - **Benefit:** Delegation between peers enhances cooperation, information exchange, and a sense of shared accountability. It reduces the likelihood of bottlenecks forming when all delegation requests are routed via a single leader. Furthermore, it allows team members to capitalize on one another's strengths, resulting in more effective job allocation.

8. **Action: Reverse Delegation Reflection**
   - **Technique:** Inspire your team to consider reverse delegation. After completing a job allocated to them, ask them to analyze the delegation process itself. What challenges did they face? Were the instructions clear? Did they require further assistance or resources? This strategy can help to enhance the delegating process.
   - **Benefit:** Delegation methods can be improved by considering reverse delegation. It encourages open communication between team members and leaders and ensures that delegation is a dynamic, ever-changing process. This feedback loop improves the overall efficacy of delegation within the company.

9. **Action: Understand Your Team's Strengths and Weaknesses:**
   - **Technique:** The first step in effective delegation is a detailed understanding of your team members' specific strengths and weaknesses. By doing a thorough skills evaluation, you can establish where each team member excels and where they may require further assistance. This data allows you to

allocate assignments that complement each team member's area of expertise, boosting productivity and results.

- **Benefit:** This strategy increases the possibility of effective results while lowering the need for extensive monitoring and reprimands by ensuring that assignments are delivered to the most qualified employees.

10. Action: Set Clear Expectations

- **Technique:** Clear instructions are essential for successful delegation. Before allocating a job or duty, schedule a one-on-one meeting with the team member who will be in charge of it. Ensure that all expectations, including the project's goals, desired results, timelines, and guidelines, are explicitly established throughout this conversation.

- **Benefit:** When everyone on the team understands their roles and responsibilities, it is simpler to minimize misunderstandings and boost the probability of a successful outcome.

11. Action: Resource Empowerment & Allocation

- **Technique:** Conduct a thorough assessment of the equipment, materials, and financing that SMEs require to thrive in their roles. Ascertain that they have access to the necessary staff, training, and technology. Without continual monitoring, SMEs should be trusted to make choices within their areas of competence. Allow them to carry out their obligations and efforts without micromanaging them.

- **Benefit:** SME performance is increased by anticipating resource requirements and empowering them via trust. This action demonstrates your commitment to supporting SMEs in prospering by instilling a feeling of ownership and responsibility in them. It also reinforces your authority and demonstrates good decision-making by exhibiting your trust in their abilities.

12. **Action: Monitor Progress Without Micromanaging**
    - **Technique:** The fact that you delegated the obligation does not exonerate you of accountability for it. Delegating effectively necessitates establishing a balance between oversight and independence. Track progress using project management tools and timely updates while respecting team members' autonomy and subject matter knowledge.
    - **Benefit:** You may stay informed and resolve any difficulties by keeping track of progress, ensuring that allocated duties are in accordance with goals without limiting initiative or uniqueness.

13. **Action: Recognition for a Job Well Done**
    - **Technique:** Implement a recognition program to acknowledge and award team members for successfully completing their assigned responsibilities in line with the leader's directions. Thank them accordingly for their dedication to and successes in carrying out their responsibilities.
    - **Benefit:** Rewarding team members for effectively completing given duties contributes to a culture of gratitude and excellence. It motivates employees to consistently perform their tasks to a high quality, boosting job satisfaction, teamwork, and overall organizational success.

Chapter Summary

Effective leaders see delegation as a time-management technique that allows them to focus on important work while also promoting the development of team member's talents. Furthermore, it promotes work-life balance, increases production, and promotes leadership development inside the organization. The capacity to grow leadership is enabled by delegating, which also empowers and motivates colleagues. Trade Secrets are covered to assist leaders in properly delegating, with an emphasis on team strengths, communication routes, appropriate resources, creating clear objectives, delegating authority, monitoring progress without micromanaging, and delivering praise and criticism.

CHAPTER 20

THE EDUCATOR'S MISSION:
SCULPTING MINDS, SHAPING FUTURES

In the grand scheme of life, educators act as guides, passing on their wisdom and experience to nurture not just knowledge but also character. They prepare individuals to continue this tradition of guidance and growth, shaping them to navigate life's complexities with resilience and insight. This influence extends across all fields, driving both individuals and businesses towards achievements in their personal and professional endeavors.

The Coffee College

Those who take on the educator role in leadership go beyond traditional authority and become mentors dedicated to the development of knowledge and abilities. Howard Schultz, a visionary entrepreneur whose influence extends beyond his stature as an inventor, is a prime example. Starbucks' innovative programs highlight Schultz's commitment to education.

The "Starbucks College Achievement Plan" was developed under Schultz's supervision. This project, in cooperation with Arizona State University, provides qualifying employees with complete tuition coverage for bachelor's degrees, regardless of their academic background. It allowed thousands of partners to further their education and established Starbucks as a preferred employer.

Schultz also announced the establishment of the "Starbucks Global Academy." Through this digital platform, Starbucks partners from all around the world may access courses on business, leadership, personal development, and career success. Schultz's dedication to enlightening minds through beneficial educational opportunities exemplifies exceptional leadership.

Howard Schultz's authority as an educator is firmly anchored in his passion for education and his personal development as a person and a corporate titan. His narrative exemplifies how leadership is more than simply imposing authority; it also entails empowering people via knowledge.

The Cultivation of Informed Decision-Making

An educator is responsible for assisting individuals in making informed decisions rather than simply presenting facts. Leaders in this position ensure that the people they lead have the knowledge and understanding needed to make sound decisions.

Consider a hospital administrator who is devoted to training their employees about the most recent breakthroughs in patient care and medical research. Because of this commitment to ongoing education, the medical team is better positioned to provide better care and make educated decisions. The administrator's strength stems from their ability to establish an environment of continuous learning and sound decision-making.

Leaders who prioritize making well-informed decisions understand the significance of information. They empower their employees with the information and resources they need to deal with difficult circumstances successfully. Their ability to lead organizations that make decisions based on facts rather than guesswork increases their authority.

Teaching Old Dogs New Tricks

Acquisition of knowledge is not time-limited; it involves the notion of lifelong learning. Intelligent leaders recognize that the pursuit of knowledge has no age limits, and that continuous education is the key to long-term success.

Leaders who believe in lifelong learning acknowledge that growth is a continuous process. They build a workforce that is eager to learn new skills and information throughout their careers by fostering a culture of inquiry and self-improvement.

But what happens when older dogs refuse to acquire these new skills? Leaders who are unable to adapt and motivate their workers to learn on a regular basis may be overtaken by their industry's rapidly changing environment. They risk losing relevance, failing to adapt to a changing reality, and ultimately failing in their efforts to become remarkable leaders. Accepting lifelong learning is more than a decision; it is frequently the difference between effective leadership, lethargy, and obsolescence.

Knowledge is Power?

Finally, a persistent willingness to learn, mentor, share, and educate is a crucial, although sometimes overlooked, trait in leadership. Genuine education emphasizes acknowledging one's limitations and the never-ending pursuit of knowledge rather than leaders portraying themselves as all-knowing or always correct. While there is no doubt that knowledge has enormous power, its actual worth is shown only when it is shared and appropriately employed. Many individuals hoard information as a form of security, but it's crucial to realize that if you're irreplaceable, you're unpromotable. Knowing that information only flourishes when it is shared and put into practice, a true leader cultivates a supportive atmosphere rather than being as inactive as an unread book accumulating dust on a shelf.

Tips & Tricks

1. **Action: Encourage Experimentation & Risk-Taking**
   - **Technique:** Create an environment in which employees are encouraged to attempt new ideas, even if they fail. Recognize and value the lessons you can learn from your errors.
   - **Benefit:** By promoting experimentation and risk-taking, a culture of creativity and resilience is promoted. Employees arc given the flexibility to examine new ideas and continuously improve workflow.

2. **Action: Expert Shadowing**
   - **Technique:** Spend time watching subject-matter experts (SMEs) in your organization. Shadow them as they go about their everyday activities, question them, and see how they make decisions.
   - **Benefit:** Expert shadowing allows you to get first-hand information and insights into their sectors. It increases your authority by demonstrating your commitment to understanding their point of view and absorbing relevant facts.

3. **Action: Employ Role-Playing for Skill Development**
   - **Technique:** Include role-playing exercises in your leadership development sessions to teach staff how to deal with a variety of situations. Create scenarios that mirror the obstacles that people might confront in their real-life roles. Assign roles to participants, such as leader and team members, and guide them through the scenario. Encourage participants to try out different techniques, make decisions, and polish their communication skills in a safe environment.
   - **Benefit:** Role-playing enhances experiential learning by allowing subordinates to apply abstract principles to real-life situations. It helps them build their abilities to solve issues,

make decisions, and communicate successfully. By immersing subordinates in realistic scenarios, they gain confidence in dealing with challenges that may arise in their positions. As participants learn from one another's perspectives and experiences, role-playing incorporates cooperation and collaboration, eventually improving your team's talents.

4. **Action: Microlearning Modules**
   - **Technique:** Create succinct, focused microlearning classes that employees may access at any time. These courses should cover specific knowledge or skill sets and be straightforward to learn.
   - **Benefit:** Microlearning supports continuous learning by breaking it down into digestible chunks. It encourages spontaneous learning and fits into busy work schedules.

5. **Action: Reverse Mentoring**
   - **Technique:** Implement a reverse mentorship program in which less experienced or younger members of the team teach leaders or senior members about emerging trends, technology, or generational behaviors.
   - **Benefit:** Reverse mentorship promotes a culture of humility and lifelong learning among leaders. It bridges generational and knowledge gaps while keeping leaders current and open to new ideas.

6. **Action: Certification & Badging Programs**
   - **Technique:** Create certification programs and digital badging systems to reward and recognize employees who reach certain training milestones or mastery of skills.
   - **Benefit:** Certification and badge programs provide employees with tangible recognition for their achievements.

They urge employees to take advantage of further learning opportunities and to grow in their skills.

7. **Action: Learning Analytics & Predictive Analytics**
   - **Technique:** Using learning analytics, you may track employee progress and engagement with training materials. Predictive analytics should be utilized to identify potential skill shortages and recommend specialized training.
   - **Benefit:** Analytics-driven insights enable HR and management to make data-backed choices on employee development. It ensures that training investments are in accordance with strategic goals.

8. **Action: Social Learning Platforms**
   - **Technique:** Set up social learning groups or platforms for employees to share knowledge, ideas, and best practices. Encourage peer-driven active involvement and learning.
   - **Benefit:** Employees may use social learning platforms to collaborate and share information. They leverage the collective wisdom of the workforce to promote education.

9. **Action: Learning Path Gamification**
   - **Technique:** Make the experience of following a learning path more interesting by including challenges, quizzes, assessments, and friendly rivalry among your team members. Create an exciting, competitive learning environment.
   - **Benefit:** Gamification boosts employee engagement and motivation. It promotes healthy competition and makes studying or achievement more enjoyable.

10. **Action: Reverse Quizzes**
    - **Technique:** On occasion, flip the script and delegate quiz creation and grading to a team leader. This not only tests

their understanding but also pushes them to assess your leadership and provide constructive feedback.

- **Benefit:** Reverse quizzes allow team members to express themselves and provide constructive criticism. By encouraging an open and cooperative culture, you demonstrate that you are willing to learn new skills from your team and strengthen your authority.

11. Action: AI-Powered Personalized Recommendations

- **Technique:** Use AI-driven recommendation engines to provide employees with pertinent courses, tools, and learning materials based on their prior performance and learning history.
- **Benefit:** By using recommendation systems based on employees' past performance and learning history, organizations can offer tailored courses, tools, and materials. This approach enhances efficiency by providing relevant resources and boosts engagement creating a more effective and personalized learning experience.

12. Action: Establish a Mentoring Program

- **Technique:** Create a structured mentoring program inside the organization that pairs seasoned employees with less seasoned employees based on skill-development needs, career goals, or special projects. Mentors should be trained and directed to ensure that they understand their roles. Create a framework for continuous one-on-one interactions, goal-setting, and progress tracking. Encourage mentees to seek advice from mentors, address difficulties, and develop goals.
- **Benefit:** Mentoring activities promote information sharing, professional progress, and a sense of community inside the organization. Mentors with vast experience give mentees useful insights, direction, and support, which speeds and

enhances their learning curve. Mentors benefit from the connection by expanding their knowledge, developing their leadership skills, and encouraging a healthy workplace culture. Mentorship programs, in general, help to expand the workforce, stimulate cooperation, and develop potential.

13. **Action: Mentor Mentees in Mentoring Skills through Role-Playing**
    - **Technique:** Be actively involved as a leader in training your mentees how to be good mentors. Engage your mentees in role-playing games in which they act out hypothetical events involving their own mentees. Encourage them to analyze different situations, create appropriate solutions, and practice communication and leadership skills under your supervision.
    - **Benefit:** Individual instruction in mentoring skills can help your mentees become successful mentors to others. Through role-playing, they may get practical experience that increases their capacity to solve problems and make decisions in mentorship contexts. This technique strengthens their leadership abilities while also improving your organization's overall mentorship program.

14. **Action: Have an Unquenchable Thirst for Knowledge**
    - **Technique:** As a phenomenal leader, cultivate an insatiable appetite for knowledge, a burning passion that motivates you to question, investigate, and acquire information and wisdom constantly. You must be hungry for knowledge, ready to discover the "hows" and "whys" that influence your surroundings. Don't just accept the status quo; actively seek possibilities for advancement and relentlessly seek solutions to create a thorough understanding of your environment. Instill this fervent desire in your team by demonstrating the value of curiosity. Encourage your coworkers to join you in this enthusiasm, transforming your company into a learning

furnace. Allow them access to educational materials and time for personal growth to help them on their path.

- **Benefit:** Accepting the burning thirst for knowledge propels your leadership with a never-ending ambition to develop and adapt. Your unlimited curiosity energizes your team, inspiring others to share your zest for investigation. Together, you will march towards an innovative and progressive future. This zealous culture builds a collective appetite for knowledge, allowing your team to take charge of their own learning journeys, propelling your business to new heights, and lighting the world on fire with your combined capacity.

Chapter Summary

The educator is critical in promoting growth, illumination, and informed advancement. This perspective crosses disciplinary borders, operating as a transformational force that guides leaders in several professions and shapes organizational futures. Leaders who take on the role of educators go beyond merely wielding authority; they become mentors, teachers, and guides dedicated to improving their colleagues' competence. Their mission is to promote curiosity and lifelong learning so that individuals may widen their perspectives. Because they know that informed decision-making is at the heart of great leadership, they equip their staff with the information and insights they require to make sound judgments. "Lifelong learning" is their slogan, and they promote a culture of inquiry and self-improvement. They build power by leading teams that are committed to constant education. Furthermore, excellent leaders integrate their personal and professional growth seamlessly, blending their values and passions into their leadership style. Finally, their leadership philosophy is based on the repetition of teaching, sharing, mentoring, leading, and learning, which fosters a culture of ongoing acquisition of knowledge and successful communication. This concept is supported by individualized learning pathways, microlearning modules, certification, and badge programs, learning analytics, social learning platforms, learning route gamification, and AI-powered tailored suggestions. Analytics, personalization, and technology are used in these ways to create a dynamic learning environment that blends employee growth with company objectives.

CHAPTER 21

TEAM BUILDING:
FROM GROUP TO GREATNESS

Team building is a thread that runs through the fabric of success. The ability to establish harmony, collaboration, and camaraderie among team members is a hallmark of exceptional leadership. This chapter examines the enormous significance of team building in leadership, looking at how it not only helps teams work better together but also helps organizations achieve their goals.

Cohesion Through Connection

The cornerstone for team building is the development of relationships among team members. Relationship-focused leaders cultivate trust and understanding among their teams. They understand that the effectiveness of a team stems from the individual abilities of its members as well as their ability to cooperate effectively.

Consider the 1980 United States Olympic Hockey Team, which is remembered for the "Miracle on Ice." This squad of university and amateur players faced a formidable battle at the Winter Olympics when fighting against the Soviet Union hockey team due to their superior talent and dominance. The U.S. American Olympic Hockey Team prioritized team development under the direction of Coach Herb Brooks. In addition to individual strengths and aspirations, they developed a culture of teamwork, sacrifice, and fraternity. The end product was a well-coordinated and very successful unit that defeated the Soviet Union and went on to win the gold medal in one of sports history's biggest upsets.

As this example highlights, teamwork is not just relevant in business boardrooms. Leaders who place a high value on team development and prioritize strong interpersonal relationships can achieve extraordinary outcomes.

Collaboration for Collective Success: A Competitive Edge

Team building seeks to maximize a group's potential in order to generate amazing results, in addition to fostering great connections. Leaders who are adept at team development understand how varied perspectives and abilities may come together to achieve innovation and success.

Pixar Animation Studios is a prime illustration of how effective leadership and teamwork can improve creative endeavors. Pixar's rise to a pioneering position in storytelling and animation was guided by visionaries such as Steve Jobs and later Ed Catmull, and was anchored by a commitment to encouraging teamwork and inclusivity. Everyone, regardless of status or expertise, was encouraged to offer ideas in this studio. This inclusive mindset not only tapped into varied viewpoints and talents but also instilled in team members a sense of worth.

Pixar's workplace was defined by an open discourse and the free flow of ideas, allowing animators, writers, and technicians to collaborate on famous films such as "Toy Story" and "Finding Nemo." Pixar's success demonstrated the importance of group achievement over individual genius, with each team member playing an important role in the creative process. Pixar's leaders intentionally implemented a risk-taking culture, striving for experimentation and innovation. The studio's accomplishments were recognized as the result of the team's mastery of the art of collaboration. Pixar's leaders didn't just cultivate creativity; they also showed how teamwork and diverse thinking could lead to collective success. They valued different perspectives and encouraged the sharing of diverse ideas.

Cultivating Resilience and Adaptability: The Power of Team Bonds

In an ever-changing environment, adaptability and resilience are essential attributes for both individuals and enterprises. Team building is an important aspect of developing these talents within a group. If team members have a tight relationship, they are more likely to weather adversity together and emerge stronger as a result.

Consider a corporate circumstance in which an organization is coping with a significant crisis, such as a financial recession or a negative PR problem. Leaders who have engaged in team development find that their teams are more resilient in such situations. These groups have surmounted problems together, have mutual regard for one another, and find strength in their group cohesion.

Johnson & Johnson's response to the Tylenol poisonings in 1982 is a brilliant example of such tenacity. The cyanide-laced Tylenol bottle incident, which resulted in seven deaths, created an unprecedented challenge for the company. However, Johnson & Johnson's leadership, which had developed an atmosphere of collaboration and confidence, came together promptly and publicly to address the situation. They altered the packaging, installed tamper-evident seals, and recalled millions of Tylenol bottles, setting a new standard for crisis management.

This image demonstrates how team building extends beyond friendly interactions to encompass the development of a trustworthy and resilient arsenal that can be employed in the event of adversity. Leaders who invest in team development ensure that their teams are not only capable of success but also have the skills to face problems head-on.

Tips & Tricks

1. **Action: Small Wins & Collaboration**
   - **Technique:** Begin by assigning a project to two departmental teams to foster cross-functional cooperation. Encourage them to work together on a project that is achievable, pleasant, and generates a positive first impression and feeling of community.
   - **Benefits:** Small successes achieved as a result of this technique create a favorable climate for future collaboration. Teams can more readily take on more difficult jobs in the future if they first create trust and rapport with an achievable and pleasurable assignment. Cross-functional cooperation enhances understanding of various departments and their functions within the organization by bridging silos. Team members expand their professional networks and learn new skills, both of which can help them grow in their careers.

2. **Action: All for One; One for All**
   - **Technique:** Incorporate the duty of establishing a happy and productive work environment into the job requirements of each team member. During interviews and orientation sessions for new employees, make it clear that the position entails not just individual activities but also the responsibility to look after their coworkers and the workspace. Instill the value of open communication, mutual support, and appreciation of one another's accomplishments.
   - **Benefit:** By explicitly defining and promoting this shared duty, you may create a culture in which every team member knows their role in keeping the workplace peaceful. This contributes to improved team cohesiveness, better job satisfaction, enhanced productivity, and overall workplace well-being.

3. **Action: Ensuring Team's Baseline Needs**
    *   **Technique:** Make certain that your team members' fundamental needs are met, much as Sun Tzu emphasized the need to ensure that troops are well-fed and compensated. Take care to ensure that your employees have regular meals, secure benefits, and fast payment of their paychecks. Implement good processes to make these tasks easier to do and to ensure that they are carried out smoothly.
    *   **Benefit:** You can build a workforce that feels valued, cared for, and supported by prioritizing the needs of your staff. This proactive approach increases their feeling of loyalty, motivation, and belonging, which boosts their performance and devotion to achieving common goals. Employees who are well-supported contribute to your team's and organization's overall performance and resiliency, much as Sun Tzu believed that well-cared-for warriors lead to victory.

4. **Action: Mix It Up; Adding Diverse Flavors**
    *   **Technique:** Many leaders feel they need to provide all the answers and ideas; great leaders recognize diverse perspectives and ideas from their team are critical for team growth. Encourage team members to share their unique thoughts and experiences. Create a welcoming atmosphere in which everyone's perspectives are appreciated and considered, regardless of their position or experience.
    *   **Benefits:** Diversity of view promotes more in-depth discussions and more innovative solutions. It encourages creativity and gives team members a sense of belonging. Teams that value diversity are more adaptable and better fitted to deal with complex issues.

5. **Action: Establish Clear Ground Rules**
    *   **Technique:** Ground rules, which are specified standards that govern team dynamics and interactions, play an

important role in building effective teamwork. Implement clear ground rules with the team, including critical topics such as communication, decision-making, dispute resolution, and more. Specific communication standards could include, for example, responding to emails within 24 hours, keeping open channels during business hours, and requiring punctuality for all meetings. Consensus-building techniques may be used in decision-making processes to ensure equal involvement. Conflict resolution strategies may encourage open communication and, if necessary, planned mediation. These ground principles not only determine how the team functions but also instill a sense of ownership and commitment among team members, resulting in a cohesive and productive work environment.

- **Benefits:** Clear and concise team standards encourage a disciplined and tranquil working environment. They decrease uncertainty, improve cooperation, and increase productivity. When everyone knows what to anticipate, team dynamics are more productive and successful.

6. **Action: Speak Up & Speak Out; Psychological Safety**
   - **Technique:** Psychological safety refers to the belief that team members may express themselves, take risks, and share ideas without fear of being evaluated or penalized. Encourage psychological safety by actively encouraging honest communication, openness, and risk-taking. Make it clear that mistakes are opportunities for learning, not causes for criticism.
   - **Benefits:** Because of psychological safety, teams may perform at their best. As a consequence, team members are more open to discussing ideas and taking calculated risks, which increases creativity and decision-making. It also promotes a culture of trust and cooperation.

7. **Action: Delegate with Empowerment**
   - **Technique:** Allow team members the freedom to decide what to prioritize in their areas of responsibility when delegating tasks or leadership roles. When guidance is needed, supply it without micromanaging. Believe in your team's strengths and empower them to take responsibility for their actions.
   - **Benefits:** When team members are empowered with both authority and responsibility through delegation, they gain a sense of personal accountability. It boosts their confidence and allows them to master new skills and make better judgments. Leaders and teams with increased authority can operate more efficiently and autonomously. When power is removed from responsibility and accountability, failure is unavoidable.

8. **Action: Team Tune-Up: Reflect & Revise**
   - **Technique:** Bring your team together on a regular basis for internal review sessions. Discuss the positive parts, the areas that may require work, and the lessons gained. Use this feedback to improve cooperation, communication, and collaboration incrementally.
   - **Benefits:** You may demonstrate your commitment to continuous development by reflecting and iterating. It allows the team to adapt and grow as situations change. Furthermore, it nurtures an environment in which everyone is given the chance to contribute to the future development of the team.

9. **Action: Define Clear Roles & Responsibilities**
   - **Technique:** Roles and duties must be clearly defined for a team to be productive. As a team builder, it is your responsibility to describe and communicate each team member's roles, including their specific responsibilities and

contributions. Make sure that roles are clearly defined and encourage team members to collaborate within them.

- **Benefit:** Roles that are carefully defined prevent overlapping or neglected duties and aid in the resolution of misunderstandings. Team members may focus on their areas of expertise, increasing output and improving workflow. It also reduces the likelihood of disputes caused by role ambiguity.

10. Action: Set Clear Goals & Objectives

- **Technique:** It is critical that your goals and objectives are specific and well-defined in order for your team to have direction and purpose. As a team builder, work with your team to develop SMART goals—Specific, Measurable, Attainable, Relevant, and Time-bound objectives. Prior to implementing, ensure these goals are consistent with the organization's overall purpose and vision.

- **Benefit:** Setting defined goals will give your staff a sense of purpose and direction. They motivate and concentrate team members to prioritize their efforts and remain committed to achieving goals. Clear goals also serve as a framework for measuring progress and performance.

11. Action: Provide Support & Development Opportunities

- **Technique:** Supporting your staff is providing them with the tools, equipment, and training they require to take care of their responsibilities. It is also critical to give opportunities for both professional and personal development. Encourage team members to gain new skills, expand their knowledge, and elevate within the team.

- **Benefit:** Giving your employees encouragement and opportunities for growth demonstrates that you care about their development. It boosts team members' competency and self-assurance, which boosts job satisfaction and morale.

Supporting their growth also raises their worth to the group and the organization.

12. **Action: Resolve Conflict Effectively**
    - **Technique:** Every team will face disagreement at some point, but how it is handled can have a significant influence. As a team builder, you must resolve difficulties promptly and efficiently. Encourage open communication to solve difficulties and, if necessary, aid with mediation. Implement conflict resolution strategies that improve communication and collaboration rather than escalation.
    - **Benefit:** Conflicts are prevented by employing effective conflict resolution techniques, which help safeguard team dynamics. It promotes a happy and productive workplace where issues are resolved peacefully. Relationships are strengthened, collaboration is improved, and the workplace is calmer as a result.

13. **Action: Recognize & Reward Achievements**
    - **Technique:** Prizes and recognition are powerful motivators for teams. Recognize and acknowledge team and individual successes on an appropriate basis. Recognize team members' efforts by recognizing them verbally, in writing, with rewards, and/or through incentive systems.
    - **Benefit:** Recognizing accomplishment develops an excellent culture and rewards good conduct. Team members are more likely to feel respected, appreciated, and, subsequently driven and motivated. Furthermore, it creates a positive feedback loop in which people and teams strive hard to achieve, which improves performance and outcomes.

Chapter Summary

This chapter underlines that outstanding leadership entails cultivating team members' harmony, collaboration, and togetherness. The core of team building is creating connections among team members because relationship-focused leaders recognize that effective cooperation is dependent not only on individual strengths but also on the ability to collaborate smoothly. The chapter also explores how team building contributes to collective success, resilience, and adaptability. This section presents actionable trade secrets, including techniques like small wins and collaboration, ensuring team baseline needs, and establishing clear ground rules. The chapter concludes by highlighting the importance of psychological safety, delegation with empowerment, team reflection, defining clear roles, setting goals, providing support, resolving conflicts effectively, and recognizing achievements in the building and sustaining of successful teams.

CHAPTER 22

THE ART OF WALKING AROUND: LEADERSHIP IN MOTION

This chapter examines the significance of Managing By Walking Around (MBWA) and why it is a hallmark of great leadership. This technique goes beyond standard hierarchical structures, providing a dynamic and nuanced approach that fosters open communication, builds trust, inspires confidence, and enhances the overall synergy within an organization. As we peel back the layers of this leadership style, we discover the keys to its effectiveness and the transforming influence it has on teams and organizational performance.

Visible Leadership and Communication: Building Trust and Connection

Leaders who can walk about become more approachable and visible, which aids in the development of a motivated and devoted workforce. Elon Musk's hands-on approach produces a strong sense of connection and belonging among his employees, whether he is testing rocket prototypes or going over vehicle design details. This technique provides Musk with invaluable opportunities to develop deeper connections with his team members and transcend his role as CEO to become an accessible resource and motivator. The enriched two-way communication and the gradual creation of trust as a result of these strengthened connections have been critical factors in Musk's success in pioneering electric vehicles and advancing space exploration.

Ear to the Ground: Listening for Insight

MBWA actively helps leaders gather first-hand feedback and listen to the pulse of their enterprise. This information is more than just data; it lays the groundwork for sensible decisions, allowing leaders to drive their organizations toward ground-breaking advances. It enables leaders to have the capacity to detect problems or bottlenecks in processes in real-time, preventing potential problems from worsening and ensuring the effective completion of their initiatives. Musk's proactive leadership style, which has been critical to the success of SpaceX missions and Tesla's production efficiency, is proven by his ability to recognize and fix these concerns before they become major issues.

Innovation: Nurturing Creative Conversations

Informal discussions during walkabouts can occasionally result in the exchange of new ideas and fixes, a technique frequently associated with Musk's leadership. His inventiveness and willingness to test out new ideas have resulted in ground-breaking innovations in the aerospace and automobile industries. For example, on one of his SpaceX walkabouts, Musk discussed rocket technology with engineers, which led to the development of the Falcon 9 rocket and the innovative concept of reusability in space travel. His dynamic leadership promotes a culture of creative thinking and continuous improvement.

Motivation: Fostering Recognition and Value

Face-to-face interactions are powerful motivators. Elon Musk, for example, took the time during a visit to the Tesla Gigafactory to personally greet and congratulate a team of engineers who had worked diligently to optimize the production process for electric vehicle batteries. He praised their innovative ideas as well as the significant boost in their manufacturing efficiency. As a consequence of Musk's recognition, the engineers felt acknowledged, which pushed them to keep coming up with new ideas to promote Tesla's goal of sustainable energy. These relationships raise spirits and inspire others to support his ambitious objectives. Team members are, therefore, driven to go above and beyond in their jobs while also feeling recognized.

Tips & Tricks

1. **Action: Inclusive Greeting Sequence**
   - **Technique:** When walking around and approaching a group, present yourself to the person with the least seniority on your team first. This might be as simple as a hello, handshake, or acknowledgment. It is important to note that this practice differs when interacting with superiors, which order is the exact opposite.
   - **Benefit:** This manner of presenting oneself gives the team a strong sense of inclusion and respect. It ensures that every team member, regardless of seniority, feels important and acknowledged. This technique encourages equality and open communication, allowing team members to share their opinions and concerns freely. Finally, it promotes a friendly and cooperative work atmosphere, increasing team trust and cohesiveness.

2. **Action: Name Calling for Success**
   - **Technique:** As you go about and talk with your coworkers, make an effort to address them by name. When you initially approach, if necessary, already have a list of the individual's names memorized, or if unplanned, attempt to sneak a glimpse at their name tags while conversing with them. Include their names when providing comments, soliciting suggestions, or expressing thanks.
   - **Benefit:** When you address your team members by name, you deepen your bond with them. It demonstrates your

admiration for and consideration for each individual as a vital contributor, resulting in a more friendly and vibrant workplace. Employee morale, motivation, and overall work satisfaction improve when they feel acknowledged and appreciated by their boss, contributing to a more productive and cohesive team. Additionally, when a person hears their name, the brain swiftly filters and prioritizes the information, diverting attention and cognitive resources toward the individual who spoke their name. This reward system, which involves neurotransmitters such as dopamine and oxytocin, contributes to the pleasurable and emotionally charged response associated with hearing one's name, reinforcing the social and personal significance of the stimulus.

3. **Action: Incorporate the "Art of War" Approach of Seeking Input**
   - **Technique:** Whenever you are on your tour, openly inquire with your employees, "What do you need? Is there anything I can do to help?" This technique corresponds to Sun Tzu's principles, which emphasize the importance of gathering knowledge and being aware of your team members' wishes and requirements.
   - **Benefit:** Seeking input from your employees helps to develop a culture of open communication and trust, similar to Sun Tzu's statement, "The finest victory is one which requires no combat." It demonstrates that you are concerned about their well-being and allows you to anticipate and respond to their needs, which enhances morale, increases production, and strengthens team cohesiveness.

4. **Action: Recognizing Achievements Publicly**
   - **Technique:** Recognize and appreciate the individual and team successes throughout your walkabouts. Express your appreciation in front of your coworkers and team members.

Praise team members publicly for their accomplishments, whether they are major milestones or minor achievements. Share success stories and recognize them for their efforts during team meetings or gatherings. Make it a practice to express gratitude to people.

- **Benefit:** Public appreciation lifts moods and reinforces a positive corporate culture. It motivates team members to strive for perfection and instills a feeling of pride in their work. Publicly congratulating team members motivates them to support and celebrate one another's triumphs, which improves team cohesion and collaboration.

5. **Action: Active Listening & Providing Timely Feedback**
   - **Technique:** Talk with the team members and listen to their concerns, ideas, and critiques. Spend some time learning about their perspectives and gathering helpful information about their work experiences with the company. Make a safe area for team members to communicate their thoughts and concerns openly. Maintain intense attention during these sessions to show that you are completely focused. Nod to demonstrate your understanding and empathy. Pose insightful questions to discover more about their opinions and recommendations. When providing feedback, strike a balance between genuine praise and constructive criticism, making sure that your comments are accurate and relevant.
   - **Benefit:** By actively listening and providing timely feedback, you build trust among your team members. When individuals feel acknowledged, valued, and supported, team morale and engagement improve. You'll also discover useful information to help you innovate and enhance cooperation and procedures. Your willingness to listen to what others have to say and respond quickly with feedback fosters an environment of open debate and continuous progress.

6. **Action: Building Relationships**
   - **Technique:** Spend some time getting to know the people on your team. In order to initiate a conversation that extends beyond work-related difficulties, inquire about their interests, hobbies, and professional objectives. With genuine attention and empathy, learn about their lives and experiences. Engage in informal conversations during your walkabouts to generate possibilities for personal connection. Inquire about significant events in their lives and remember essential details. Pay attentively and show empathy when team members express their stories.
   - **Benefit:** Developing great relationships with your team members builds a sense of trust and camaraderie inside your firm. It generates a friendly workplace climate in which team members feel valued and encouraged, which improves teamwork and idea-sharing. These bonds encourage more commitment and devotion, which increases work satisfaction and retention.

7. **Action: Promoting Cross-Departmental Interaction**
   - **Technique:** Encourage cross-departmental interactions during your walkabouts. Create opportunities for team members from other departments to communicate, share ideas, and collaborate. Organize informal get-togethers or meetings that bring people from varied backgrounds and perspectives together. Participate in these sessions, contributing your ideas to the discussion and creating a feeling of collaboration across departments.
   - **Benefit:** Encourage cross-departmental involvement to promote creativity and problem-solving by using your whole organization's aggregate expertise and abilities. It breaks down barriers and encourages collaboration, resulting in new ideas and a more peaceful workplace.

8. **Action: Problem-Solving On the Spot**
   - **Technique:** Take care of any little problems or challenges that arise throughout your rounds. Use your presence during walkabouts to identify and point out issues but aim to resolve the concerns to show your engagement and willingness to collaborate. To come up with feasible ideas together, encourage open conversation, and request feedback from team members. Ensure that everyone involved understands their roles and responsibilities in putting these ideas into action.
   - **Benefit:** Proactively resolving concerns during walkabouts lowers interruptions and maintains a good work atmosphere. They will have more trust in your leadership since it demonstrates your dedication to supporting your team. Collaborative problem-solving versus "hit-and-run management" (when a manager drops off problems in the workplace and then leaves without assisting) develops a sense of loyalty and accountability among team members, resulting in a more robust and adaptable workforce.

9. **Action: Leading by Example**
   - **Technique:** Model the attitudes and work habits you want your employees to have throughout your walkabouts. Demonstrate devotion, professionalism, and a strong work ethic in your own activities and responsibilities. Make it apparent that you are committed to your responsibilities. Accept challenging assignments, meet deadlines regularly, and uphold the organization's standards and principles. Show resilience and a hopeful mindset in the face of adversity.
   - **Benefit:** Setting a positive example for your team to emulate raises the bar. It creates a culture of excellence and responsibility by inspiring others to emulate your dedication and work ethic. When team members see their manager

actively promoting the company's values and goals, they are more likely to feel motivated and enjoy their work.

10. Action: Strategic Inspections & Observations

- **Technique:** Strategic inspections should be a key component of your MBWA approach. As you interact with your team or department as normal, keep an eye on operational components such as procedures, tools, and workspaces. Investigate methods to increase organization, safety, and efficiency. Discuss in depth with team members to understand their experiences and any issues they may have in doing their duties.

- **Benefit:** Strategic inspections allow you to detect and fix operational issues ahead of time while also demonstrating your dedication to a productive work environment. This hands-on engagement imparts open communication and cooperation among your team members, as well as the development of a culture of continuous growth. By refining operations based on your observations and team feedback, you boost morale, productivity, and overall performance. As your leadership presence becomes connected with proactive problem-solving and assistance, your MBWA strategy gains traction.

Chapter Summary

The focus of this chapter is on a critical component of effective leadership, as encapsulated in the concept of Managing By Walking Around (MBWA). This leadership style goes beyond traditional hierarchies, emphasizing dynamic and nuanced interactions that foster open communication, trust, confidence, and overall organizational synergy. The importance of visible leadership, the art of listening, driving innovation, motivating through recognition, and practical actions such as inclusive greetings, name calling for success, seeking input, publicly recognizing achievements, active listening with timely feedback, building relationships, developing cross-departmental interaction, on-the-spot problem-solving, leading by example, and strategic inspections and observations are all discussed in this chapter. Through direct and personal engagement, each action is strategically designed to improve leadership effectiveness, team morale, and organizational performance.

CHAPTER 23

THE SCIENCE OF TIME MANAGEMENT
THE LEADER'S HOURGLASS

Time is both a finite and valuable resource. How effectively a leader controls their time has a significant impact on their leadership effectiveness, productivity, goal attainment and reputation. This chapter investigates the critical importance of time management in increasing productivity, decision-making, overall success, and the ability to multitask efficiently.

Efficiency: The Driving Force

Effective time management is the key to organizational efficiency. Leaders with this skill may simplify their operations, eliminate time-wasting tasks, and utilize every second. As a consequence, activities are completed on schedule, and resources are employed efficiently in the well-oiled engine of a company.

As an example, consider Jack Welch, the former CEO of General Electric (GE). Welch is known for having outstanding time management skills. He put in place a framework that required GE's business units to be top or second in their respective markets, with a constant focus on efficiency, which is the essence of time management. This emphasis on efficiency propelled GE's growth, and it also helped Welch establish himself as one of the most successful CEOs in corporate history.

For leaders who know that their ability to maximize each day affects not just their personal productivity but also sets the tone for their whole business, time management is a major responsibility. An effective leader inspires others to be productive by building a culture in which time is valued and used wisely.

Informed Decision-Making: The Power of Prioritization

Effective decision-making is at the heart of leadership, and time management is critical to this process. Effective time managers make mental room for scenario analysis, option weighing, and decision-making.

Warren Buffett, the famed investor and CEO of Berkshire Hathaway, is an example of a leader who excels in managing time for decision-making. Buffett's daily schedule is well-known for its focus and simplicity. He makes time for reading and contemplation, which allows him to assess investment choices and make sound financial decisions. His tight time management methods have had a significant impact on his achievement.

Leaders who prioritize time management have the advantage of being able to focus their attention on the most critical tasks. They avoid the traps of getting mired down in trivial tasks or allowing others to rule their agendas. Because of this level of time management, they are able to make decisions that are compatible with their strategic aims and principles.

Goal Achievement: Turning Vision into Reality

Visionaries and leaders set high standards and inspire others to do the same. These ambitious goals, however, may only ever be aspirational without effective time management. Time management is the connection between vision and reality.

Elon Musk, of SpaceX, Tesla, the Boring Company, Solar City, Neuralink, xAI, and X (formerly called Twitter), is a live example of how time management can help you achieve your goals. Musk is known for his relentless work ethic and incredible ability to handle many projects at once. His technique comprises setting specific time periods for various activities, allowing him to make significant progress on his lofty goals. SpaceX's groundbreaking space travel achievements, Tesla's innovation in the electric vehicle sector, the Boring Company's tunneling projects, his solar company's advancements in sustainable energy, his groundbreaking advancements in brain-computer interfaces through Neuralink and artificial intelligence, and his profound influence on free speech through his communication platform on X have all benefited from this meticulous time management.

Effective time managers may assist leaders in transforming lofty goals into manageable tasks. They break down large amounts of work into tiny portions, plan their time carefully, and make steady progress toward their goals. This not only boosts their personal performance but also drives their employees to work vigorously and meaningfully toward common goals.

Balance and Well-Being: The Leader's Self-Care

Leadership is a challenging profession that may quickly lead to burnout if time management is overlooked. Effective leaders understand that time must be made for both personal and professional responsibilities.

Richard Branson, the creator of the Virgin Group, is well-known for his spirit of adventure and ability to balance work and personal life. Despite his numerous business ventures, Branson has always emphasized the need to make time for leisure, family, and relaxation. His ability to achieve this balance has contributed to his longevity as a successful businessman and leader.

Leaders who respect time management also prioritize self-care. They recognize that their physical and mental health have a direct impact on their ability to lead effectively. They maintain the energy and resilience needed to lead effectively over time by making time for rest, relaxation, and personal interests.

Tips & Tricks

1. **Action: "Not-To-Do" List**
   - **Technique:** In addition to your to-do list, keep a "not-to-do" list. This list contains procedures or behaviors that you consciously restrict or avoid in order to save time. Excessive social media use, meaningless meetings, and difficult yet pointless work are just a few examples.
   - **Benefits:** Making a "not-to-do" list allows you to keep track of chores that may interfere with your productivity. It assists you in maintaining discipline and concentrating on tasks of the highest importance, reducing time spent on needless or distracting activities.

2. **Action: "Eating the Frog"**
   - **Technique:** Doing your most difficult or unpleasant task first thing in the morning is referred to as "eating the frog." By finishing the most difficult activity first, you may remove mental clutter and boost your confidence for the rest of the day.
   - **Benefits:** The most difficult work should be prioritized at the start of the day to ensure it gets the attention it deserves. It puts an end to procrastination and sets the tone for the rest of the day.

3. **Action: The Pomodoro Technique**
   - **Technique:** The Pomodoro Technique requires working for focused intervals of time—typically 25 minutes—followed by a quick break of 5 minutes. Following the completion of the four periods, take a longer respite of 15 to 30 minutes. During each concentrated phase, avoid distractions and maintain complete attention.
   - **Benefits:** The Pomodoro Technique promotes sustained attention and production. You may avoid burnout and maintain a high level of attention by breaking your job into reasonable timepieces. This method can help you improve your time estimating skills by allowing you to forecast how long activities will take more precisely.

4. **Action: Apply the 2-Minute Rule to Email**
   - **Technique:** To the two-minute rule, add email management. If you can respond, assign, or complete the required task in two minutes or less after opening an email, do it immediately. Set designated time intervals to address emails that require additional time rather than replying to your inbox continually throughout the day.
   - **Benefits:** The 2-Minute Rule may be used to reduce distractions and keep your inbox orderly. This strategy guarantees that brief answers are handled quickly, saving time and reducing email overload. Dedicated time frames for longer responses enable you to concentrate on other tasks, eliminating worries about your reply and creating an environment free from distractions for focused work.

5. **Action: Perform Regular Time Audits**
   - **Technique:** As part of your periodic time audits, track your time consumption for a week or more. Sort your activities into categories such as work-related, personal, social media, and recreational. Examine the results to identify time wasters

and areas where you may change your approach to work more efficiently.

- **Benefits:** Time audits provide valuable information regarding your time management strategies. They aid you in identifying patterns, areas for growth, and opportunities to reallocate time to other useful pursuits.

6. **Action: Strategic Mindfulness & Time Blocking**
   - **Technique:** Combine time management and mindfulness activities. Begin each work session with a simple mindfulness practice to help you focus and clear your thoughts. Then, employ time blocking to set up specific intervals for work to ensure that you are completely engaged and present during those times.
   - **Benefits:** Time blocking and mindfulness both help you stay present and engaged at work. They improve focus, reduce stress, and foster a sense of purpose during working hours.

7. **Action: Eisenhower Matrix; Prioritize Tasks**
   - **Technique:** Priorities must be established in order to manage time effectively. Determine your most important responsibilities at the start of each day and prioritize them. Use tools such as the Eisenhower Matrix to classify activities into four quadrants: urgent and important, important but not urgent, urgent but not important, and neither urgent nor important.
   - **Benefit:** Setting priorities allows you to focus your efforts and time on the things that are most important and influential. You may achieve your goals with less stress, and without feeling overloaded. As a consequence, you will be able to manage your time better.

8. **Action: Set SMART Goals**
   - **Technique:** Set SMART goals (Specific, Measurable, Attainable, Relevant, and Time-bound). By keeping clear objectives in mind, you can stay on track and ensure that your tasks are in accordance with your broader aims. Divide large, complicated goals into more realistic, smaller milestones to make advancement more reachable.
   - **Benefit:** SMART goals provide direction and clarity. They bolster your drive and sense of purpose. By breaking down big goals into smaller, manageable milestones, you can track your progress and celebrate achievements along the way.

9. **Action: Delegate & Collaborate**
   - **Technique:** Delegation is an effective time management method. Assign tasks that can be completed by others to members of your team or coworkers.
   - **Benefit:** Effective delegation empowers your team members and encourages their growth while freeing up your time to focus on high-priority assignments. Collaboration allows you to leverage your strengths as a group, increases productivity, and develops a feeling of shared accountability.

10. **Action: Use Technology Wisely**
    - **Technique:** Make use of technology to help you manage your time better. Use a calendar and task management software to keep your schedule and to-do lists organized. Set up notifications and reminders for important deadlines and meetings. Examine productivity, video conferencing, and time management solutions designed to improve your workflow.
    - **Benefit:** Using digital tools and applications helps to enhance organization, automate repetitive tasks, and simplify

procedures. This saves time while also lowering mistake rates and improving data management.

Chapter Summary

Time management science is critical for good leadership. The control of time, a finite and irreplaceable resource, is critical for leaders to be efficient, make sound decisions, achieve their objectives, and maintain a healthy work-life balance. Controlling time allows leaders to manage workflows, conserve mental space for well-informed judgments, and transform high goals into actionable strategies. Leaders who employ methods like "Eating the Frog," "Not-To-Do" lists, and the Pomodoro Technique may navigate the obstacles of their roles with focus and discipline. This chapter stresses the importance of time management in improving leaders' effectiveness and encouraging their teams to attain success and well-being.

Section IV

Advanced Leadership Techniques

Welcome to Section IV: Advanced Leadership Techniques, where we dig into the finer points of leadership. We'll look at advanced leadership concepts in this section, such as how to form exceptional teams through interviews and the Kaizen approach to continuous growth. Before uncovering the concealed power of financial fluency, we'll also investigate the intricate combination of art and science that happens in strategic negotiation. Join us as we seek to grasp these cutting-edge strategies and lay the groundwork for leadership mastery.

Chapter 24

Kaizen:
The Path to Continuous Improvement

Kaizen acts as a road map for advancement and excellence in the ever-changing world of leadership and professional development. Kaizen, a Japanese concept that means "constant improvement," has transformed industries and grown into a foundation for both individual and communal growth. This chapter examines the Kaizen concept, looking at its philosophy, applications, and revolutionary influence on leadership.

The Essence of Kaizen

Kaizen is a concept that promotes small, incremental improvements. It opposes quick, drastic change in favor of gradual development. The essence of Kaizen is the belief that little adjustments, when combined together, may result in significant breakthroughs. It is a mode of thinking that promotes an environment of continuous learning, adaptation, and progress.

The Kaizen Principles

To understand Kaizen fully, it's essential to grasp its fundamental principles:

- **Continuous Improvement:** The primary principle of Kaizen is a commitment to constant improvement. It stresses the fact that we must continuously develop to become more efficient.
- **Standardization:** Kaizen encourages the development of standardized processes and procedures to eliminate inconsistency and inefficiency.
- **Elimination of Waste:** Waste, whether in the form of time, resources, or effort, is the adversary of production. Kaizen reduces waste via rigorous examination and improvement.
- **Employee Involvement:** A critical element is one that employees at all levels may identify chances for improvement and actively engage in the process.
- **Problem Solving:** A key component of Kaizen is the emphasis on spotting problems, investigating their causes, and developing innovative solutions.

Adopting the Kaizen philosophy as a leader provides various advantages for establishing a culture of continuous improvement inside teams and businesses. The first approach is to lead by example when executives who are actively working on improvement projects inspire their employees to do the same. Employee involvement in the improvement process not only results in better solutions but also increases engagement and work happiness. Furthermore, Kaizen principles may have a significant impact on strategic planning, ensuring that long-term corporate goals and a commitment to continuous improvement are aligned. Kaizen is a problem-solving process that executives may employ to improve operational efficiencies or resolve team disagreements. Furthermore, Kaizen promotes regular feedback exchanges and open communication, which generates a transparent and collaborative work environment.

A Real-Life Example

Take, for example, Toyota, a prominent participant in the automobile sector that has long used the Kaizen approach. Kaizen is the core of Toyota's production system, often known as the "Toyota Way." One of the most well-known aspects of this method is the practice of delegating authority to factory floor workers to halt the manufacturing line if they see a flaw. This demonstrates Kaizen in action, in addition to ensuring the highest quality.

The Transformative Impact

Professional growth and leadership benefit greatly from Kaizen. It enables leaders to preserve a competitive edge, adjust to change more effectively, and promote an inventive and resilient culture. By adopting Kaizen, leaders and organizations may reach their full potential and embark on a road of continuous development and improvement.

Tips & Tricks

1. **Action: Implement Lean Principles**
   - **Technique:** Adopt Lean principles, a management philosophy derived from the Toyota Production System (TPS), such as value stream mapping, the 5S Methodology (sort, set in order, shine, standardize, sustain), and continuous flow to decrease waste, eliminate unnecessary stages, and simplify operations.
   - **Benefits:** Lean strategies enhance resource usage, save costs by reducing waste, and improve overall effectiveness by focusing on tasks that provide value. They result in quicker turnaround times, higher production quality, and more productivity. Lean principles promote a culture of continuous improvement.

2. **Action: Data-Driven Decision-Making**
   - **Technique:** Use measurements and statistics to evaluate performance and make sound decisions. Use key performance indicators (KPIs) and conduct performance evaluations on a regular basis.
   - **Benefits:** Using data-driven decisions, you may discover patterns, identify bottlenecks, and track progress toward improvement goals. As a result, more effective problem-solving approaches have evolved, yielding better results. It also encourages accountability and transparency inside the organization.

3. **Action: Cross-Functional Teams**
   - **Technique:** Form cross-functional teams comprised of members from several departments to work on specific improvement projects. Assign specified tasks and responsibilities to each team member.
   - **Benefits:** Cross-functional teams bring a range of perspectives and subject matter knowledge to the table. They stimulate collaboration, demolish silos, and produce new solutions by using your workers' aggregate expertise. These groups usually generate significant and long-term gains.

4. **Action: Continuous Training & Development**
   - **Technique:** Investing in ongoing training and development activities can help your personnel enhance their skills. Determine skill gaps and provide training to address them.
   - **Benefits:** Continuous learning keeps your team up to date on industry best practices. It leads to a more adaptable team and higher levels of employee work satisfaction. Employees with current skills can also contribute more significantly to the organization's attempts to develop continuously.

5. **Action: Standardize Processes**
   - **Technique:** To ensure organizational consistency, the technique entails not only establishing but meticulously documenting work procedures and best practices, with a focus on providing specific instructions and performance benchmarks, resulting in the creation of a comprehensive framework that serves as a guide for employees to follow in their day-to-day tasks. Creating extensive process manuals, holding employee training sessions, and performing frequent performance assessments to guarantee adherence to defined criteria are examples of actions within this technique.
   - **Benefits:** The meticulous documenting of methods and benchmarks guarantees that jobs are completed with high accuracy and regularity, eliminating the possibility of errors or deviations. This improves organizational efficiency while also serving as a significant resource for employee training and onboarding. The benefit of developing a standardized framework extends to greater employee confidence and proficiency, promoting a work environment marked by precision, dependability, and overall elevated performance.

6. **Action: Kaizen Events & Workshops**
   - **Technique:** Hold frequent Kaizen workshops or events where teams focus intensely on process improvements. Set defined objectives and goals for each event and devote time and resources to achieving them.
   - **Benefits:** Kaizen events accelerate the process of improvement by concentrating attention and resources on specific areas. They instill a sense of urgency, yield quick successes, and keep your drive for continuous improvement on track. Kaizen events provide a controlled environment for teams to communicate and execute changes quickly.

7. **Action: Implementing Kanban**
   - **Technique:** Implementing the Kanban method, a practical Visual Task Management technique, can help organizations improve workflow efficiency. This entails visualizing tasks on a Kanban board and classifying them into columns labeled "To Do," "In Progress," and "Completed." This streamlined method allows for improved prioritization, reduces bottlenecks, and maintains a controlled workflow.
   - **Benefit:** Regular team meetings to evaluate the Kanban board encourage transparency, collaboration, and continual improvement. Kanban implementation provides a visual, adaptive, and collaborative technique for effectively managing activities. This succinct but powerful method adds to the overall improvement of organizational workflow efficiency.

8. **Action: Encourage Employee Feedback**
   - **Technique:** Create a culture in which workers are encouraged to provide feedback on workflows and procedures. Establish periodic feedback techniques, such as suggestion boxes, questionnaires, or team meetings, to gather their ideas.
   - **Benefits:** Employee input is crucial as frontline workers typically serve as the primary identifiers of opportunities for change. Additionally, encouragement of employee feedback via a feedback culture and periodic techniques promotes continuous development and increases employee engagement. Actively seeking frontline workers' perspectives nurtures an environment in which employees feel appreciated, aiding in the identification and resolution of problems and creating a feeling of ownership, all of which contribute to constructive organizational development.

Chapter Summary

The Japanese philosophy of Kaizen, which means "constant improvement," acts as a guidepost for the ever-changing world of leadership and professional growth. This chapter delves into the ideas of Kaizen, emphasizing the need for continuous progress over quick, drastic change. Kaizen concepts like standardization, waste reduction, employee engagement, and issue resolution provide leaders with the tools they need to foster a culture of continuous learning, adaptability, and development within their teams and organizations. Embracing Kaizen provides leaders with the resources they need to drive innovation and resilience while maintaining competitiveness and agility. Organizations and leaders may attain their full potential and embark on a road of continuous development with the support of this idea. Trade Secrets provides actionable strategies for successfully incorporating Kaizen concepts into leadership and professional development, such as encouraging employee involvement, implementing Lean and Kanban methodology, making data-driven choices, forming cross-functional teams, and hosting Kaizen events.

CHAPTER 25

THE GAME OF INTERVIEWING: CRAFTING EXCEPTIONAL TEAMS

The Guardian

Few skills are more important in leadership than the ability to conduct effective interviews. Having good interviewing skills is the first step in assembling successful teams, cultivating talent, and ultimately attaining organizational excellence. It's fascinating to note that, despite the importance of interviews, most leaders go on this critical journey with little to no preparation. Active listening, body language analysis, behavioral and situational questions, mirroring, generating cognitive dissonance, utilizing active deception, and even the delicate art of deceit detection will all be covered in this sector.

Interviews are more than just casual conversations; they are vibrant interactions in which potential, ability, and character are evaluated and disclosed. They are similar to a thrilling game in which contestants compete against one another. As a leader, you have the dual responsibility of curator and guardian, maintaining and preserving the culture of your organization. In this exciting game of interviewing, you have the option to select the winning strategy, constantly striving for exceptional personnel to ensure your company's successful development.

Consequences and Impact

Ineffective interviews may have negative consequences. A bad hire can lead to low team morale, waste of resources, lower production, and even legal action. The actual cost extends beyond money; it has an influence on your company's well-being and inhibits the attainment of strategic goals.

As a leader, making the correct judgments is crucial, as is selecting the proper team members. Excellent interviewing skills help you to make smart judgments while aligning your personnel with the values and objectives of your firm. Your leadership effectiveness will improve, and your objective will become more reachable if you surround yourself with skilled, driven, and culturally suitable people.

Tips & Tricks

1. **Action: Strategic Questioning**
   - **Technique:** In order to conduct an effective interview, you must ask meaningful questions. In addition to analyzing their qualifications, it requires developing insightful interview questions that probe deeper into a candidate's motives, character, and problem-solving skills. Instead of "Tell me about your abilities" or "What makes you right for this job," you may ask, "Can you offer an example of a difficult scenario when you failed and how you overcame it?" or "What research have you done regarding our firm and this position to have prepared you for this interview?"
   - **Benefit:** Strategic questioning throughout the interviewing process offers several advantages. It, first and foremost, allows interviewers to gain deeper insights into candidates' qualifications, character, and problem-solving skills in order to make more informed recruiting judgments. By asking questions that elicit answers that go beyond the surface level,

interviewers can more properly identify a candidate's suitability for the role and the firm. Furthermore, it demonstrates that the organization values insightful remarks and encourages applicants to emphasize their unique skills and experiences. As a result, the company's reputation as a top employer may increase, attracting top talent.

2. **Action: Employ Shocking Questions**
   - **Technique:** Include unique and thought-provoking interview questions, such as "What are the reasons I should 'not' hire you?" or "What is the most innovative initiative you implemented, and how did you follow through on it?" and "Why not?" if they did not pursue it. If they have not implemented any innovative ideas, ask a follow-up question: "Why haven't you? Is that indicative of your management philosophy?" and, "How do I know you can be innovative then?". These questions are designed to catch candidates off guard and encourage open discourse that shows their self-awareness, flexibility, and honesty.
   - **Benefits:** Through surprising questions, candidates are challenged to think critically and analyze their experiences. They give insight into a candidate's ability to respond to unanticipated events calmly and honestly. Encourage candidates to discuss their weaknesses or failings to learn more about their self-awareness and openness to learn and improve. Furthermore, when presented with surprising queries or other unexpected scenarios during an interview, applicants' natural instinct is to offer rapid, unfiltered replies to subsequent questions, frequently divulging facts they had hoped would not be brought up. They feel compelled to act in order to regain their footing and make a positive first impression. This candor can provide useful information about their thought processes, decision-making abilities, and

communication style, improving the overall evaluation of their appropriateness for their role.

3. **Action: Active Listening**
   - **Technique:** Active listening is paying considerable attention to tone, intonation, and nonverbal clues in addition to hearing. Active listening is a tactic used by skilled interviewers to absorb not just the words themselves but also the intricacies of the applicants' delivery.
   - **Benefit:** This approach detects nuances and provides a better understanding of a candidate's personality and communication preferences. Leaders may learn a lot about a candidate's suitability for the job and the culture of the organization by watching both the verbal and nonverbal components of their replies. As a result of smarter recruitment decisions, the appropriate people are paired with the right jobs.

4. **Action: Observation & Body Language**
   - **Technique:** Include observation in your interview process, paying attention to nonverbal cues and body language. During the interview, pay close attention to the seven crucial body language indicators listed below:
     - i. **Eye Contact:** Examine a candidate's ability and consistency in making eye contact. Consistent and appropriate eye contact typically indicates interest and self-assurance. Avoiding eye contact, on the other hand, might indicate discomfort, shyness, or even dishonesty.
     - ii. **Facial Expressions:** Examine a candidate's facial expressions for signs of real emotion. Smiles may indicate delight, while frowns might convey discomfort or discontent. Additionally, be attentive to micro expressions, brief, involuntary

facial expressions that can reveal hidden emotions and provide valuable insights into a candidate's true feelings.

iii. **Posture:** Examine the candidate's posture; an open, upright stance shows confidence and attention to detail. Defensive or slouching attitudes, on the other hand, may imply discomfort or apathy.

iv. **Hand Gestures:** Examine the frequency and purpose of hand gestures. Excessive gesticulation may indicate anxiety, whereas purposeful, controlled movement enhances communication. Sporadic fidgeting might also suggest anxiety when answering specific questions.

v. **Mirroring:** Observe if candidates subtly mirror your body language during the interview. Mirroring, where individuals unconsciously match communication styles, can suggest a sense of rapport and engagement, fostering a more positive and collaborative interview atmosphere.

vi. **Nodding:** Take note of any candidates that nod in agreement during the interview. Nodding frequently indicates that someone is listening and agreeing with what you're saying. Excessive or meaningless nodding may be interpreted as insincerity.

vii. **Touching Face or Neck:** Examine whether a candidate often touches their face or neck. These behaviors, while not necessarily suggestive of dishonesty, might be explained by defensive mechanisms, fear, or discomfort, necessitating more investigation.

- **Benefits:** When you add observation and body language analysis into your interview process, you boost your ability to evaluate applicants properly. It provides useful information about their actions, answers, and genuineness. Adding nonverbal cues to your hiring decision criteria might help you locate candidates who not only have the requisite abilities but also fit with your company's culture and values. This thorough evaluation method assists in both the establishment of successful working relationships and the formation of stronger, more cohesive teams.

5. **Action: Behavioral & Situational Questions**
    *   **Technique:** To understand more about a candidate's problem-solving talents and prior experiences, use behavioral and situational interview questions. Unlike hypothetical questions, these ones require candidates to offer specific examples of their actions and accomplishments. As an example, you may ask someone, "Could you explain a circumstance in which you were entrusted with leading a team during a crisis?" or "How did you rate the situation's success, and what was the outcome?" Base the questions discreetly on the demands of the role and your company.
    *   **Benefits:** Behavioral and situational interview questions might help you evaluate applicants more effectively. Learning about their real-life experiences can help you better understand how they have overcome hurdles and contributed to their previous duties. This technique will help you forecast how they will perform for your firm. Furthermore, it allows you to locate professionals who not only have the necessary credentials but also a track record of effectively using their skills. Finally, employing this method allows you to make better hiring decisions and pick people who will fit well with your team and corporate culture.

6. **Action: Build Rapport with Mirroring**

   - **Technique:** During interviews, use mirroring to develop rapport with applicants. Mirroring involves mimicking the candidate's body language, tone, and communication style. This strategy seeks to inspire applicants to relax and participate more completely in the interview by developing familiarity and comfort. It's critical to note that mirroring does not imply copying; rather, it entails forging a bond based on empathy and understanding.

   - **Benefits:** Mirroring can increase the candidate's entire interview experience and degree of comfort. When candidates are at ease, they are more likely to open up and provide honest comments. You may have more successful and informative conversations with the aid of this method, which will help you evaluate candidates' appropriateness for the role and the firm. Developing rapport via mirroring helps candidates have a positive experience regardless of the outcome of the recruiting process. Even if the candidate is not hired, your organization will be perceived as one that values interpersonal skills and effective communication as a result of this method.

7. **Action: Active Deception Detection**

   - **Technique:** Using active deception detection throughout the interview process, you can uncover abnormalities or warning indicators in a candidate's replies. Making informed recruitment decisions requires not just starting with the assumption that applicants are speaking the truth but also keeping a lookout for any signs of deception.

     Common Deception Indicators: Keep an eye out for various deception indicators, including:
       i. **Inconsistent Statements:** Candidates may provide contradictory information or change

their replies in response to queries posed at various times throughout the interview.

ii. **Avoidance of Specifics**: Dishonest applicants may employ unclear language or try to avoid providing particular information when questioned about their former experiences, making it harder to verify their answers.

iii. **Excessive Defensiveness:** Candidates who demonstrate extreme defensiveness, deflection, or dispute when challenged about their qualifications or history may be concealing something.

iv. **Non-Verbal Cues:** Pay attention to nonverbal cues such as nervous laughing, sweating, or fidgeting, as these physical markers may indicate discomfort or possible dishonesty.

v. **Storytelling vs. Truth:** Dishonest candidates usually rely on memorized, prepared comments that may lack emotion, sincerity, or real-life context. Genuine remarks typically include personal anecdotes and detailed facts.

vi. **Overemphasis on Positives:** Some applicants may overstate their achievements or positive characteristics in order to divert attention away from any possible flaws or limitations.

vii. **Lack of Self-Reflection:** Candidates who are dishonest may struggle to explain their previous mistakes, flaws, or deficiencies. They may be eager to blame outside influences rather than accept responsibility for their conduct.

Being aware of these signals might help you determine whether a candidate is being entirely honest. However, these deception detection strategies must be used with caution and in conjunction with other interview techniques. False positives can have a detrimental influence on the candidate's experience and cause them to miss out on opportunities.

- **Benefits:** Active deception detection allows for the selection of persons who not only meet the standards but also demonstrate integrity and honesty, which are vital for developing a trustworthy and ethical work environment. It helps you minimize the risks that might result from hiring someone who exaggerates their talents or motivations. By detecting deception early, you may avoid costly recruiting mistakes while also preserving your company's trust and image.

8. **Action: Building Trust & Comfort**
   - **Technique:** Conducting interviews that generate a sense of ease and trust is essential for making effective and moral employment decisions. It requires creating a pleasant interview setting that reflects your leadership style and communicates your commitment to treating people fairly and with respect, which may have a long-term impact on your firm's image. Consider the following critical elements to do this:

     i. **Effective Communication:** Candidates should be fully informed about the interview process, including expectations and timeframes. Keep them informed at every stage of the journey.
     ii. **Respectful Environment:** Create an environment that respects applicants' uniqueness, privacy, and time. Make certain that interviewers are always courteous and professional. Don't put up with interruptions; turn off your phone's ringer and forward your office phone.

     iii. **Openness to Questions:** Encourage applicants to ask questions and provide honest, transparent answers. This promotes an open-dialogue culture.

     iv. **Feedback:** When feasible, specifically with internal candidates, provide constructive feedback regardless of the outcome to help candidates progress.

     v. **Timeliness:** Respect the candidates' schedules by arriving on time. Long waits and delays can make individuals uneasy and erode their confidence.

     vi. **Follow-Up:** Stay in touch with applicants after interviews and follow up as quickly as possible to keep them informed about the hiring process and maintain their interest. This demonstrates your respect for their candidacy and the process.

- **Benefits:** Building trust and comfort during interviews not only allows you to make better-informed hiring decisions but also improves your company's image and brand. Candidates who loved their interview experience are more likely to endorse your company even if they are not hired. Furthermore, it sets the tone for their future engagement, whether as customers or employees.

9. Action: Establish a Welcoming Environment

- **Technique:** Create a calm interview environment that emphasizes order, comfort, and the lack of distractions. As they approach your interview location, greet them warmly, identify yourself, and walk them through the interview process in detail. This first welcome is critical in putting candidates at ease as soon as they arrive.

- **Benefits:** Aside from the interview, having a pleasant environment generates a positive reputation for your firm. It demonstrates a strong commitment to a welcoming and polite recruiting process. Remember that for many prospects, this is their "first day on the job" and their first engagement with your company. The impression you create at this critical juncture will last a lifetime. Candidates are more likely to offer their best effort when they feel appreciated and at ease, which may help you more correctly assess their talents and potential fit with your organization. This technique fosters inclusion and a sense of belonging, enhancing your company's reputation as a great place to work.

10. **Action: Active Listening & Respect**
   - **Technique:** Demonstrate to the candidate that you actually care about what they have to say throughout the interview. Encourage them to share their expertise, thoughts, and experiences. Maintain a courteous and compassionate dialogue while paying great attention and following up with queries. If they bring up beliefs and points of view that differ from your own, there is no need for debate, make notes, and move on to the next question.
   - **Benefit:** Candidates appreciate active listening and respect. They have a better experience because they are made to feel valued and listened to. This method not only boosts your company's reputation but also promotes open discussion and trust, which raises the probability that candidates will think highly of your company even if they aren't recruited. When confronted with opposing opinions, engaging in a debate may inadvertently provide individuals with the responses you seek, potentially influencing their subsequent answers to align with your perspective in an effort to please or conform.

11. **Action: Employing the "Awkward Pause" Technique**
   - **Technique:** When conducting interviews, employ the awkward pause approach to convince applicants to react deliberately. This starts with asking a tough question and

then stopping to allow the interviewee time to think and respond. If they struggle, do not break the silence. This method is especially useful when applicants are not prepared to answer the question or are hiding something. Following such queries, expand the tactic by asking follow-up questions like "Anything else?" or "Can you give me another example, this time with an unsuccessful outcome?"

- **Benefits:** Using the awkward pause technique during interviews has many benefits, including:
    i. **Discomfort and Honesty:** When there is a long wait following a question, a candidate may feel uncomfortable or pressed to answer. During this uncomfortable phase, candidates typically open up more in an attempt to win over the interviewer. They may express sentiments, ideas, or experiences that they would ordinarily hide or sugarcoat in a short response. When there is a long, uncomfortable pause, they tend to be franker and more honest.
    ii. **Reduces Scripted Responses:** Before an interview, candidates might prepare and rehearse responses to common issues, resulting in scripted or polished responses. This intended technique, however, is shattered by the Awkward Pause. Candidates are less likely to employ prepared responses since they don't know when you'll break the pause. They are more likely to respond with honest, real perspectives and experiences.
    iii. **Enhances Spontaneity:** Because silence makes candidates uncomfortable, candidates are more inclined to speak up in the heat of the moment without overanalyzing or filtering their comments. This spontaneity can lead to more

genuine and unanticipated replies, which portray a more realistic picture of the applicant.

iv. **Reveals Problem-Solving Skills:** Candidates who can handle and capitalize on silence demonstrate flexibility and problem-solving abilities. They display the ability to deal with tough or unexpected situations with calm and sincerity.

12. **Action: "Don't Give Away the Answers to the Test."**

- **Technique:** Most interviewers "overshare" when it comes to wording their questions. During the interview, avoid providing the candidate with any information that may influence them only to make replies that are consistent with the information you have provided. Once you've concluded that the applicant is a good fit, wait until the conclusion of the interview to reveal the position and the accompanying expectations. Example:

  i. **Bad Question (Oversharing):** "You will be in control of a team of five individuals working on a large customer project in this job. This job will be challenging due to the project's demanding customers, limited deadlines, and lack of teamwork. Could you tell me about how you lead your team?"

  ii. **Good Question (Open-ended):** "Could you describe a tough project you recently worked on, how you solved it, and how you measured the effectiveness of your efforts?"

  iii. The interviewer provides too much information on the position, the group, and the obstacles in the 'bad" question. As a consequence, the applicant may elect to revise their response to better reflect the information presented. The

271

experienced interviewer keeps the topic open-ended so that the candidate may draw on personal experience and respond more candidly.

- **Benefit:** This technique ensures that applicants are evaluated based on their real abilities and qualities rather than simply repeating what you just told them. When you delay specific information until after the evaluation is completed, you maintain the validity of the assessment while also creating trustworthiness. It reduces the possibility that candidates may change their responses to fit a predetermined narrative or expectation. Finally, strategic transparency benefits both the organization and the applicants by saving time and money and ensuring a complete and unbiased examination.

13. Action: Addressing Discrepancies & Inconsistencies

- **Technique:** During the interview, be proactive in highlighting any discrepancies or abnormalities in the interviewee's résumé or replies. Point out any errors or discrepancies you notice in a polite but confident manner, asking for clarification or an explanation of the differences. Encourage the interviewee to provide context for their answers or to correct inaccuracies in their supporting materials or responses. A good follow-up question in this scenario would be, "In consideration of these mistakes on your resume, how can I be confident in your abilities to ensure attention to detail as a leader?"

- **Benefit:** Addressing resume gaps and discrepancies has various advantages. For starters, it allows you to assess the interviewee's genuineness and moral integrity, which are important attributes for any prospective team member. Second, it allows the candidate to offer any legitimate causes for the anomalies, such as changes to job tasks or responsibilities. Last but not least, it demonstrates your commitment to in depth investigation as well as the importance of truth and transparency inside your organization. This technique builds trust, ensures that you employ wisely, and promotes honesty and openness norms within your team.

14. Action: Team Feedback Inquiry

- **Technique:** Request feedback from multiple team members who interacted with the candidate in various positions following the interview, such as the receptionist, office staff, or HR officials. During these interactions, especially those that were not technically part of the recruiting process, ask questions about the applicant's behavior, attitude, and professionalism. Encourage team members to be open and honest about their observations.

- **Benefit:** A team feedback inquiry gives a comprehensive understanding of the applicant's interpersonal skills and interactions with various people inside the firm. This strategy assists in the finding of valuable information that may be missed during formal interviews. It ensures that the candidate behaves consistently, professionally, and correctly in all interactions, demonstrating their real character and qualification for the post. Furthermore, it reinforces the company's commitment to an open and collaborative recruiting process, establishing a positive reputation and culture.

15. Action: Post Interview Communication

- **Technique:** It is vital to maintain open and productive channels of contact with candidates during the interview process. After the interview, for internal candidates, offer feedback that highlights both their strengths and places for growth. Be transparent and honest about the impending procedures and deadlines for the recruitment process. For career-focused and leadership jobs, it is reasonable to expect a follow-up thank-you contact from the candidate. Allow them a 24-48 hour opportunity to initiate this contact before following up.

- **Benefit:** Throughout the interview process, open communication and the use of constructive criticism display professionalism and respect. This method fosters a pleasant applicant experience, which may lead to them recommending your company to others. Furthermore, it indicates your dedication to moral behavior, which enhances your reputation as a leader and promotes the company's perspective. The candidate's willingness to initiate communication following the interview can disclose information about their interest and involvement, but the candidate's lack of contact may be cause for concern.

16. **Action: Establish Transparent and Consistent Social Media Screening Policies**
    - **Technique:** Create clear policies for using social media in the hiring process to ensure transparency and consistency. Before accessing applicants' social media content, obtain their explicit consent. Seek legal counsel to ensure compliance with privacy and anti-discrimination laws. Evaluate social media content based on job-related criteria, emphasizing non-discriminatory factors.
    - **Benefit:** Organizations promote trust, reduce legal risks, and create a fair and equitable recruiting process by implementing transparent and consistent social media screening rules. Informed consent displays respect for applicants' rights, while legal counsel assures regulatory compliance. Emphasizing job-related factors improves recruiting decision objectivity, lowering the likelihood of discrimination claims and creating a favorable candidate experience.

17. Action: Invest in Mastering the Interviewer's Toolkit

- **Technique:** To become a great leader in interviewing, seek thorough training and development that covers all aspects of this skill, such as human behavior analysis, linguistics for effective communication, question framing and progression, resume deciphering, interrogation techniques, negotiation skills, technological screening, recruitment strategies, and the nuanced craft of deception detection.

- **Benefit:** Developing your interviewing skills can help you become a more successful leader by enabling you to construct high-performing teams and develop exceptional individuals, both of which are essential components of effective leadership. With a comprehensive arsenal at your disposal, you'll master the art of selecting the best individuals, ensuring your company's ultimate ascension. Your expertise will contribute to an extraordinary culture that attracts top talent, stimulates innovation, and keeps you up to date on current trends and best practices. Regular practice and information development can boost your confidence in conducting outstanding interviews, and using technology and tools will expedite the process, saving time and resources. Finally, by recruiting and selecting the best people, your dedication to excellence in interviewing will significantly contribute to the success of your firm and set it on a path to greatness.

Assessing Candidate Behavior in Interviews

When picking applicants, it is vital to recognize that candidates typically perform at their best during interviews; thus, keep this in mind while conducting them. If a candidate acts inappropriately during an interview, this raises major issues. If their conduct does not match your expectations at this moment, it is typically improbable that it will alter later. As a result, executives must recognize when to reject a candidate who does not meet their company's criteria and goals, even if they look exceptional on paper. It is critical to make the right decision throughout the interview process if you want to put together a team of people who share your values and ideas.

Chapter Summary

Mastering the art of effective interviewing is a critical skill in the realm of leadership. The importance of utilizing interviews as crucibles for properly analyzing potential, competency, and character is emphasized in this chapter. Inadequate interviewing can harm team morale, available resources, and overall productivity. Excellent interviewing skills enable leaders to make sound judgments, ensuring that team members selected align with the organization's principles and objectives. This congruence makes the vision more attainable, which promotes leadership effectiveness. Active listening, body language analysis, behavioral and situational questions, mirroring, generating cognitive dissonance, and utilizing active deception detection are among the interviewing techniques covered in this chapter. It is underlined that building trust and comfort during interviews is critical for conducting moral and effective evaluations, encouraging openness, and avoiding prejudice and discrimination. Recognizing that candidate conduct during the interview is a reflection of their prospective alignment with company values emphasizes the importance of making informed selections during the interview process.

Chapter 26

Strategic Negotiation: Merging Expertise & Science

Learning how to bargain effectively is akin to knowing how to utilize a strong instrument to alter the direction of your organization. Negotiation skills are critical for leaders, whether they are building connections, resolving difficulties, or making strategic decisions. In this chapter, we'll look at the underlying importance of negotiation as well as a variety of overt and covert tactics for improving your deal-making talents.

The Essence of Negotiation

Negotiating successfully entails reaching mutually beneficial agreements via debate and compromise. Your ability to properly bargain may have a direct impact on your organization's effectiveness as a leader. It includes striking a balance between achieving your goals and cultivating relationships. Creating value for both parties is more essential in a negotiation than simply getting what you want.

The Consequences of Ineffective Negotiations

Consider the consequences of unsuccessful negotiations. Poor negotiation skills may lead to failed agreements, damaged relationships, and missed opportunities. Leaders who are inept at negotiating may unknowingly hurt their organizations by leaving potential value on the table or jeopardizing critical alliances.

The Impact on Leadership

Leadership and negotiation go hand in hand. Effective leaders are often skilled negotiators who can guide their teams to victory. Negotiation skills may help you make smart decisions, settle disagreements, and develop cooperative relationships. Because of them, you may confidently conquer challenging hurdles and embrace possibilities.

Consider Nelson Mandela, the prominent leader who was essential in putting South Africa's apartheid system to an end after nearly five decades. Mandela's ability to cope with the apartheid state, which had long oppressed the majority of people, displayed his diplomatic talents.

Nelson Mandela used a multifaceted approach in his discussions to end apartheid, demonstrating his effective leadership and diplomatic talents. Mandela's unshakable dedication to reconciliation was a major pillar of his negotiation technique. Instead of seeking vengeance or retaliation for the apartheid regime's years of oppression, Mandela advocated for forgiveness and peace. This commitment not only served to reduce tensions but also laid the groundwork for a more inclusive and harmonious South Africa post-apartheid.

Furthermore, Mandela stressed the importance of trust-building throughout the negotiation process. Recognizing the country's significant mistrust amongst different racial and ethnic groupings, he took conscious steps to create a climate in which trust could be reestablished. Mandela's personal integrity and consistency in fighting for a unified South Africa were critical in garnering the trust of all parties involved in the negotiations.

Mandela also displayed a unique capacity to achieve win-win situations, stressing outcomes that benefited all parties involved. This attitude was dramatically different from a zero-sum worldview, in which one side's gain was regarded as the other's loss. Mandela's vision for a democratic South Africa was based on collaborative solutions that addressed both the oppressed majority's demands and the minority's fears.

Mandela's negotiating skills were thus crucial in allowing a peaceful and gradual transition to democracy. His leadership throughout these vital conversations not only averted the possibility of violent conflict but also opened the path for South Africa to become a more just and equitable nation. Mandela's legacy in negotiation exemplifies the transforming power of principled and inclusive leadership in the face of seemingly insurmountable obstacles.

Tips & Tricks

1. **Action: Preparation & Information Gathering**
   - **Technique:** A thorough preparation is required for all successful negotiations. Before commencing any negotiation, it is critical to conduct extensive research and accumulate essential material. Understanding the parties involved, their interests, and, most crucially, your own goals is a necessary step. The better you grasp the negotiating environment, the more you can effectively construct compelling arguments and counterarguments during the negotiation process.
   - **Benefit:** Careful planning provides you with information and insight, providing you with a tactical advantage in negotiations. It allows you to anticipate the other party's movements, identify areas of agreement, and make compelling proposals. This level of preparation boosts your ability to accomplish solid results and make beneficial relationships through effective negotiation.

2. **Action: Learning Poker for Negotiation Skills**

   - **Technique:** To increase your negotiation skills, learn the art of playing poker. In poker, learn how to read other players, assess the situation, and take measured risks. Learn to bluff by becoming aware of when to fold and when to press your advantage. Learn how to analyze risks, calculate odds, and keep your cool under pressure.

   - **Benefits**: Poker can teach you essential negotiating skills. Understanding an opponent's tells, for example—subtle clues that suggest their intentions—is akin to determining a person's secret aims in negotiations. Poker bluffing may teach you when and how to employ strategic deception to your advantage, similar to how to use negotiation methods to influence outcomes in your favor. Furthermore, learning poker enhances your capacity to spot dangers, allowing you to analyze and manage risks during negotiations properly. Overall, poker provides a dynamic setting for improving negotiating skills that may be applied in a variety of leadership and decision-making scenarios.

3. **Action: Harness the Home Field Advantage**

   - **Technique:** In the same manner that Sun Tzu's "The Art of War" emphasizes the need to use one's position or surroundings to gain an advantage, apply this approach to negotiations and dispute resolution. Control factors such as time, location, emotions, and support systems to ensure you have the upper hand. Plan the bargaining atmosphere strategically to favor your goals. Choose occasions when you are well prepared, and the conditions are good. Choose a setting that is both comfortable and favorable to constructive talks. Maintain calm while putting the other person off balance having to manage emotions. To solidify your position, assemble the necessary support, whether it's people with essential knowledge or a strong data analysis team.

- **Benefit:** By adopting Sun Tzu's "home field advantage" principle, you position yourself for negotiation success. Controlling the negotiating atmosphere helps you to set the tone, increasing your chances of success. You'll be more confident and collected, equipped to tackle difficult discussions and disagreements, whether through time, location, or emotional management. Furthermore, having the correct assistance reinforces your position and decision-making, guaranteeing that you are well-equipped to achieve beneficial outcomes.

4. **Action: Active Listening**
   - **Technique:** Active listening is a fundamental skill required for effective negotiating. It includes paying close attention and fully comprehending what others are saying. Attentively monitor their speech and nonverbal cues to learn about their perspectives, needs, and worries. Additionally, identify what they are not saying or topics they are avoiding.
   - **Benefit:** Active listening is a talent that may assist both sides in a negotiation in feeling understood, identifying their plan, and gaining the trust of the other. It allows you to identify areas of agreement and similar interests or areas of weakness, making it easier to devise solutions that benefit both sides. Furthermore, it increases communication and reduces misunderstanding, allowing for more fruitful talks and stronger working collaborations.

5. **Action: Setting Clear Objectives**
   - **Technique:** A well-defined strategy is required for effective negotiating. Before beginning any talks, it is critical to establish clear and defined objectives to be addressed and to stay away from. This means defining your goals in terms of

tangible outcomes while also considering the larger picture consequences on your relationship with the other person.

- **Benefit:** A real and tangible checklist, as well as clearly stated objectives, will assist you in staying focused on your goals throughout negotiations. They reduce the likelihood of wandering off course or succumbing to pressure that isn't in your best interests. By having a strong sense of purpose, you increase your chances of achieving your desired results while maintaining the integrity of your broader goals.

6. Action: Creating Value

- **Technique:** Negotiators that are effective recognize that negotiations are about expanding the pie rather than merely dividing it to benefit all parties. Look for opportunities to uncover shared interests and innovative solutions that may benefit everyone. By taking a collaborative approach and exploring win-win circumstances, you may boost the total value of your conversations.

- **Benefit:** Negotiation abilities that add value strengthen connections and collaboration. It develops goodwill among parties and demonstrates your commitment to finding reasonable solutions. This method builds long-term, profitable connections while also improving the probability of reaching peaceful agreements.

7. Action: Leveraging BATNA

- **Technique:** If negotiations fail to yield a good outcome, your best alternative to a negotiated agreement (BATNA) acts as a backup plan. In conjunction with leveraging BATNA, having well-thought-out contingency plans adds another layer to your negotiation strategy. These plans detail specific measures and responses in the event that talks take an unexpected turn or if your core goals cannot be fulfilled through the initial agreement.

- **Benefit:** Knowing your BATNA offers you negotiating leverage and certainty, allowing you to determine whether to back out of a contract that does not suit your interests. A clear BATNA allows you to bargain from a position of strength. It establishes a clear standard against which to assess prospective agreements and determine whether they deliver higher value. By successfully applying your BATNA, you improve your ability to secure more beneficial agreements and avoid settling for inferior outcomes.

8. **Action: Building Trust**
   - **Technique:** Trust is required for productive discussions. Credibility must be established via sincerity, transparency, and consistency. Gain trust by promoting open communication, reducing outward displays of disrespect, and promoting collaboration—all of which are critical components of effective negotiations.
   - **Benefit:** In negotiations, trust fosters cooperation and goodwill. It creates an environment in which both parties feel comfortable exchanging facts and contemplating new views. When there is trust, negotiations are more likely to proceed smoothly and yield mutually beneficial solutions. This opens the door to potential long-term collaborations based on trust.

9. **Action: Adaptability & Flexibility**
   - **Technique:** Negotiations are intrinsically diverse, and each situation necessitates a distinct approach. Recognizing that the methods used in internal departmental negotiations (which are the majority of the subject of this chapter) may differ dramatically from those utilized in Wall Street high finance. Good negotiators are adaptable and flexible in their strategic preparation. This also entails being aware of the subtleties of each negotiation, comprehending the individual

dynamics at work, and being prepared to alter methods, approaches, and ideas as needed. It also entails admitting that you may approach a negotiation with a specific strategy only to learn that you need to adjust it dynamically to maximize outcomes.

- Benefit: Negotiation adaptability and flexibility boost your ability to overcome unexpected roadblocks and seize fresh opportunities. It allows you to react tactically to shifting dynamics, increasing your capacity to attain desired goals. It also demonstrates your agility and commitment to finding solutions that please all sides, resulting in more successful and effective talks.

10. Action: Master the Art of Deception

- **Technique:** Make use of the Art of War's deception approach. This tactic, which is based on Sun Tzu's idea that "All combat is founded on deception," is deceiving your team or opponents by subtly concealing certain facts or intentions while revealing only the specifics required for the task at hand. You must also be aware that your adversary may be using the same tactic.

- **Benefit:** By mastering the art of deception, you can confuse opponents and rivals and prevent them from correctly predicting your actions, in accordance with Sun Tzu's principle of "Encircling an army without allowing a route is not a good idea. Don't put too much pressure on an agitated foe." This allows you to keep the upper hand in negotiations, preserve a feeling of surprise, and make better-informed judgments without undue outside influence.

11. Action: Emotional Intelligence

- **Technique:** The finest negotiators can read and regulate their own emotions as well as the emotions of others. They understand how emotions influence decision-making and utilize this knowledge to bargain successfully. They may steer talks toward more beneficial results by recognizing when emotions are building and using techniques to lessen tension.

- **Benefit:** Emotional intelligence in negotiation leads to more collaborative and fruitful conversations, as well as more agreements that benefit both sides. It promotes the building of rapport and trust with counterparts, which may lead to better and more long-lasting commercial relationships.

12. Action: Silence as a Tool

- **Technique:** Experienced negotiators recognize the significance of quiet. They use it deliberately to urge the opposite side to speak up, supply more information, or modify their viewpoint. For example, imagine negotiating the terms of a business purchase, and after presenting your proposal, you intentionally pause, allowing the silence to create a space for the other party to express their feedback or potentially reveal aspects of their strategy that they might not have revealed otherwise.

- **Benefit:** When employed as a technique, silence might urge the opposing side to make further concessions and divulge sensitive information. It helps negotiators to actively listen to and grasp the counterpart's point of view, resulting in better-informed decision-making.

13. Action: Strategic Concessions

- **Technique:** Great negotiators know when and how to make strategic concessions. They understand that not all issues are equally valued and are willing to make concessions on minor issues in order to gain an edge over major ones. This technique demonstrates versatility while protecting critical interests.

- **Benefit:** Strategic compromises can result in more productive talks by fostering collaboration and goodwill.

They allow negotiators to create rapport with their opponents and discover points of agreement, which eventually leads to mutually advantageous agreements.

14. Action: Negotiating in Stages

- **Technique:** Instead of seeking to address all issues at once, effective negotiators usually break difficult conversations into stages. As a consequence, they may deal with simpler issues first and build rapport before moving on to more difficult ones. Furthermore, it may give opportunities for minor triumphs and compromises.

- **Benefit:** Staged negotiations provide an ordered and regulated negotiation process. It improves the chances of attaining individual issue agreements, building momentum, and maintaining a positive attitude throughout the negotiation, all of which lead to more successful outcomes.

15. Action: Leveraging Time Pressure

- **Technique:** Effective negotiators understand how time limits impact their decision-making skills. They might use deadlines or generate a feeling of urgency to persuade the opposite party to make compromises or reach an agreement. Timing may be a highly powerful instrument in negotiations.

- **Benefit:** Using time limitations can help to speed up talks and result in faster resolutions. It encourages counterparts to achieve speedy agreements and compromises, reducing the chance of lengthy, pointless discussions and ensuring that opportunities are not missed.

16. Action: Identifying Negotiation Techniques

- **Technique:** Recognize that effective negotiation is a multifaceted skill that requires strategy mastery as well as knowledge of potential strategies used by your adversary. Notice that your opponent may use similar or more techniques, making it critical to recognize and respond to them accordingly.

- **Benefit:** Learning bargaining methods enhances your ability to navigate difficult negotiation scenarios successfully. You get a strategic edge by being aware that your competitors may employ similar strategies. This knowledge enables you to anticipate their maneuvers, alter your approach, and successfully employ countermeasures. Finally, having a diverse set of abilities will help you stand out as a skilled negotiator who can succeed in challenging and competitive negotiations.

Chapter Summary

Throughout the chapter, the capacity to create mutually beneficial agreements via conversation and compromise, with an emphasis on coordinating goals and developing relationships, is emphasized. The chapter stresses the underlying link between leadership and negotiation, as well as the wide-ranging consequences of ineffective negotiations, such as failed deals and strained relationships. Principles such as reconciliation, creating trust, and seeking win-win solutions are demonstrated in real life by Nelson Mandela's negotiation skills. Planning and data gathering, active listening, setting precise goals, creating value, utilizing BATNA, establishing trust, adaptability, and flexibility, emotional intelligence, strategically using silence, making strategic concessions, negotiating in stages, and taking advantage of time pressure are also covered. These techniques are critical for leaders who wish to succeed in the negotiating process.

Chapter 27

Financial Fluency:
A Leader's Secret Weapon

The ability to handle and comprehend numbers is a sometimes underappreciated skill that may make or break a leader's road to success. A detailed grasp of budgets, expenditures, revenues, and financial intricacies is critical for leaders who wish to drive their companies toward profitability. This chapter examines the need for financial literacy in leaders, the strategic use of budgets as a tool for achieving goals, and the role that financial awareness plays in effective leadership.

The Vitality of Numbers in Leadership

Leaders who are financially knowledgeable have a great tool at their disposal to carry out their objectives. Statistics, according to these leaders, are more than just spreadsheets and data; they are the foundation for making strategic decisions. Leaders may quantify their goals, measure progress, and make choices based on data. Effective leaders who navigate the financial environment understand that the majority of corporate challenges have an economic underpinning.

Budgets as Tools, Not Constraints

In the arena of leadership, budgets are commonly misunderstood. Some see them as necessary evils, while others see them as limitations. Budgets are extremely useful tools for progressive leadership. A well-structured budget will help your master plan succeed. It provides a financial roadmap defining available resources and how they should be dispersed. Remember that if you don't own your budget, it will own you. Effective leaders see their budgets as useful allies, aiding them in successful goal attainment.

When leaders utilize their budgets as tools, they gain several benefits. Firstly, budgets enable leaders to correctly allocate resources, ensuring that the appropriate investments are made where they are required. This not only keeps the organization financially stable but also boosts its potential for development and innovation.

Secondly, budgets allow managers to track progress more effectively. By comparing actual outcomes to planned quantities, leaders may identify disparities in financial performance and act promptly to remedy them. This enables executives to stay on track toward their goals and make educated decisions.

Thirdly, budgets are critical for risk management. They help decision-makers anticipate and plan for financial challenges. With a well-planned budget at their disposal, leaders can confidently manage unanticipated obstacles and make necessary modifications.

A Real-World Example

As an example, consider Jack Welch, the renowned former CEO of General Electric (GE). Welch was well-known for his command of number-driven environments and his ability to make effective use of statistics. He established a "vitality curve" performance evaluation system at GE, which awarded employees a performance score. Welch utilized this strategy to influence his judgments on promotions, increases, and layoffs by using data and figures. GE saw tremendous growth during his tenure as a consequence of his meticulous attention to the minutia of the business and his leadership abilities.

Cranial Calculations: Impressive Problem-Solving

In the corporate world, numbers are used to solve issues and make choices. Outstanding leaders can effortlessly do challenging calculations "in their head," which advances their problem-solving abilities and reputations. They dissect difficult issues, conduct rapid calculations, and assess feasible solutions using their mathematical skills. This competence demonstrates their meticulous attention to detail, providing workers and stakeholders with the certainty that their decisions are supported by careful study and immediate consideration.

Furthermore, these executives position themselves as the financial stewards of their organizations, with a full understanding of financial accounts, projections, and budgets. This expertise not only aids in problem-solving but also in effective financial management, which promotes the financial health of the organization.

Tips & Tricks

1. **Action: If You Don't Own Your Budget, It Will Own You**
   - **Technique:** Recognize that the greatest time to advocate for your budget and financial priorities is before the budget development process, not during it, and markedly not after. Begin proactive talks and strategic planning meetings with your finance team and the essential stakeholders far before the budget is prepared. Declare your vision, goals, and financial requirements clearly to ensure that they align with the forthcoming budget cycle. Work with your finance team to ensure that the budget structure includes your objectives.

- **Benefit:** By handling budget planning in a proactive manner, you position yourself as a leader in control of financial choices. You may decide how monies are prioritized and resources are deployed to achieve your goals and vision because of your strategic foresight. Furthermore, it reduces the likelihood of falling into financial challenges or problems once the budget has been approved. Early communication and planning ensure that your financial needs and strategic goals will be met. It's critical to remember that managing the numbers also entails influencing budget development to ensure you achieve your leadership goals.

2. **Action: Shadow Finance Teams**
   - **Technique:** Spend some time observing your accounting and finance personnel at work. Learn firsthand about financial reporting, analysis, and processes.
   - **Benefit:** Immersion in financial operations delivers real insights into the financial health of your firm. It allows leaders to make better-informed decisions and effectively engage with financial specialists, building strong relationships.

3. **Financial Benchmarking Tours**
   - **Technique:** Organize benchmarking visits in which executives visit companies known for having great financial management. Analyze their financial practices, strategies, and cultural aspects.
   - **Benefit:** Through benchmarking trips, leaders are exposed to diverse financial innovations and practices. They supply fresh insights and ways that may be changed to improve your company's financial savvy.

4. **Action: Deciphering Financial Triumph**

   - **Technique:** Examine the breadth of financial successes, both within and outside of your industry. Reverse engineering the strategies and decisions that propelled companies to financial success is a journey worth exploring. For example, assume you are the CEO of a technology startup. By examining the financial performance of a well-established IT giant, you may find critical strategies such as product diversification and a strong emphasis on customer retention. Then, you may apply your discoveries to your own company, researching new product prospects and enhancing consumer interaction tactics.

   - **Benefits:** Examining financial success stories may disclose a plethora of information. As a manager, you may modify and use tried-and-true strategies in your own company or industry, increasing financial performance and directing your team to success.

5. **Action: Scenario Proformas**

   - **Technique:** Create financial scenario simulations for your firm (pro forma). Model the implications of various financial situations on budgets, revenues, and expenses. These simulations can include a variety of scenarios, ranging from optimistic growth forecasts to more conservative estimates, allowing for a full evaluation of alternative outcomes.

   - **Benefit:** Scenario simulations, which improve decision-making, enable executives to forecast financial outcomes in a variety of circumstances. They prepare leaders to respond to changing market conditions in a profitable manner.

6. **Action: Financial Mentorship**

   - **Technique:** Request coaching or partnering with CFOs or other experienced financial experts. Develop relationships with mentors and mentees to obtain specialized teaching.

- **Benefit:** Financial coaching provides specific advice and insights. It facilitates leaders' financial awareness by connecting them with seasoned financial advisors.

7. **Action: Competitor Financial Analysis**
   - **Technique:** If possible, and in an appropriate manner, compare your firm's measurements to those of your rivals by doing extensive financial analyses of their financial goals, metrics, and performance indicators.
   - **Benefit:** Through specific competitor financial research, you find opportunities for development and learn about industry benchmarks. Executives may use this strategy to tailor financial strategies to current market trends, providing your organization with a competitive advantage.

8. **Action: Financial Literacy Workshops**
   - **Technique:** Schedule financial literacy training programs for your team and leadership. Explain essential financial statements, concepts, and measures.
   - **Benefit:** Financial literacy workshops help managers and employees throughout the firm to communicate in a common financial language. This increases teamwork and informed decision-making at all levels.

9. **Action: Excel Proficiency for Effective Leadership**
   - **Technique:** Microsoft Excel is a versatile tool for organizing, analyzing, and making choices. Begin with learning the essentials, such as creating spreadsheets, entering data, and doing simple calculations. Progress to more advanced capabilities like pivot tables, macros, and data visualization. Practice often and consider enrolling in online seminars or tutorials to enhance your skills.

- **Benefit:** Excel proficiency provides executives with a key skill set for making informed decisions and successfully managing data. It allows you to automate internal company activities, analyze complex data, and make data-driven choices. Excel proficiency enhances your leadership abilities and will enable you to make more informed decisions, whether you're managing budgets, project timelines, or performance metrics.

Cranial Calculations Tricks for Doing Math in Your Head:

10. Action: Chunking Numbers
- **Technique:** Divide complex computations into smaller, more manageable chunks. Divide a large number into smaller pieces, multiply those parts separately, and then sum the results.
- **Benefit:** Chunking not only minimizes cognitive strain, making mental computations easier, but it is also an effective strategy for improving accuracy. The chance of errors is reduced by breaking difficult computations down into smaller, more manageable parts. This is especially useful in situations when precision is essential, such as financial analysis or scientific computations. Chunking thus not only alleviates the mental stress of dealing with complex numbers, but it also contributes to the general reliability and precision of the calculating process.

11. Action: Round & Adjust
- **Technique:** Round numbers to the nearest multiple of 10 or 100, then apply the appropriate changes to the result. When calculating percentages, for example, round integers to multiples of 10%.

- **Benefit:** Aside from the advantage of simplifying computations and enabling faster mental calculations, the round and adjust strategy is especially useful in situations when precision is not the major objective. This method is useful when a short estimate or approximation is sufficient for decision-making. Rounding and adjusting, for example, provides for a more efficient evaluation of trends and patterns without becoming bogged down in complicated numerical minutiae when evaluating huge datasets or doing early financial assessments. This technique strikes a balance between speed and precision, making it a useful tool for situations requiring a quick but reasonably accurate estimate.

12. **Action: Estimation & Proportion**
    - **Technique:** Estimate values to come close to them. For example, to find 16 percent of a value, first find 10% and then divide it by half.
    - **Benefit:** Estimation simplifies mathematical challenges so that they may be handled mentally. It is especially useful when accuracy is not required.

13. **Action: Practice Mental Visualization**
    - **Technique:** Picture numbers and processes in your thoughts when you perform math. Create an "equation" or diagram in your head to help you visualize the operation.
    - **Benefit:** You may improve your mental math talents by providing computations with a visual framework that makes them easier to solve.

14. **Action: Mental Math Games**
    - **Technique:** Play games and do other activities to improve your mental math skills. Some examples are Sudoku, mental math puzzles, and math speed tests.

- **Benefit:** Mental math games make arithmetic more fascinating and engaging while also enhancing your calculating speed and accuracy.

Chapter Summary

Numbers quantify leaders' success; they go beyond just simple digits. Financially aware leaders who view budgets as tactical tools have a distinct edge. They efficiently navigate their enterprises, seamlessly overcome financial challenges, and use budgets as a beacon illuminating the path leading to the realization of their mission. Effective financial leadership necessitates a full awareness of budgets, expenses, revenues, and the complexities of corporate finances. When a leader thoroughly grasps the notion of financial control, they can utilize it as a powerful tool to make educated decisions that will lead their businesses to success.

CONCLUSION

MAKE A TOAST TO LEADERSHIP EXCELLENCE

Let's raise a glass as we bring the final chapter of "Trade Secrets - A Reference Guide To Leadership Excellence" to a close. This isn't just a celebration of completing a book; it's a toast to the profound strategic lessons and methodologies we have uncovered on this journey.

As you begin to implement the goals and tactics denoted in these pages, keep in mind that you now have a comprehensive toolset of skills and standards to help you improve your leadership abilities. Your development will be nothing short of revolutionary, and those you lead will undoubtedly go through transformative experiences as a result of your mastery of these leadership concepts. Here is to becoming the extraordinary leader you were born to be, armed with the trade secrets that will propel you to the top. Cheers to your continued leadership journey!

In typical Chapter Summary fashion, here is a quick snippet of each chapter of your leadership journey:

1. **Integrity:** Maintain unwavering ethical standards to establish a foundation of trust that will last beyond adversities.

2. **Authority:** Develop your ability to use influence appropriately, balancing encouragement and guidance while maintaining moral responsibility.

3. **Hard Work and Humility:** Adopt a strong work ethic, align your efforts with those of the corporation, and stay motivated and humble.

4. **Communication:** Improve your communication skills to inspire, connect, and inform your team.

5. **Decisiveness:** Make sure you and your team are constantly on track by making appropriately timed decisions, maintaining clarity, and leading with confidence.

6. **Vision & Creativity:** To direct your organization toward a brighter future, be courageous and think "huge," both creatively and strategically.

7. **Adaptability, Toughness, & Problem-Solving:** Overcome challenges, encourage innovation, and strengthen your company's resilience.

8. **Courageous Confidence & Resolving Conflict:** support the values of effective leadership, fostering a trustworthy and productive environment.

9. **Cool, Calm, & Collected:** Keeping your calm under pressure will make your team members feel more comfortable and confident.

10. **Leading by Example:** Lead your team by setting the example, inspiring and motivating them through your actions.

11. **Resilience & Thick Skin:** Gain the ability to overcome hurdles and look at challenges objectively, which will help you solve difficulties and improve.

12. **Enthusiasm:** Infuse your leadership with dynamic energy to motivate and excite your team.

13. **Vigor:** Being tenaciously committed and dedicated to greatness will help you and your company advance.

14. **Approachable:** Increase trust and inclusion among your team members by being open and respectful with one another.

15. **Empathy:** Use the power of understanding to strengthen your bonds with your team and drive progress.

16. **Inspire:** Set an example, empower your staff, encourage creativity, and recognize successes to build a healthy work environment.

17. **Laughter:** Make the workplace more fun, stress-free, and human through humor and laughter.

18. **Micro to Macro:** Strike a balance between paying attention to details and contemplating the larger picture to make smarter judgments.

19. **Effective Delegation:** Empower your team by delegating tasks and decision-making while maintaining ultimate accountability for results.

20. **The Educator:** Develop your team's knowledge and abilities while encouraging a culture of inquiry and ongoing development.

21. **Team Building:** Create trustworthy connections among your team members to encourage synergy, resilience, inventiveness, and cooperation.

22. **Art of Walking Around:** Direct contact with your employees will increase morale, stimulate feedback, and promote ongoing development.

23. **Time Management:** Learn the science of time management to boost productivity, make sensible decisions, and maintain a good work-life balance.

24. **Kaizen:** Develop a culture that encourages flexibility and inventiveness, as well as gradual development and innovation.

25. **Effective Interviewing:** Conduct in-depth strategic interviews to assess individuals' potential, talents, and moral character while ensuring organizational standards are followed.

26. **Negotiation:** Reach mutually beneficial agreements through debate and compromise, goal coordination, and networking.

27. **Financial Leadership:** Recognize budgets as tactical tools for accurately and financially guiding your firm.

These chapters, which are overflowing with useful tips and trade secrets, have served as your compass on your journey of leadership. Applying these ideas diligently can assist you in creating outstanding leadership experiences that will have a beneficial, long-term influence on your teams and organizations. May your leadership serve as a sign of everlasting excellence, leaving an indelible imprint on both your institutions and the individuals you have assisted along the way. The time is now to create your leadership legacy.

* * *

AUTHOR BIOGRAPHY

Kevin J. Peterson, a distinguished luminary in the hospitality and resort industry, brings an illustrious 40-year career to the forefront of leadership excellence and innovation. Kevin's journey in leadership began with humble roots, and he has since forged an extraordinary career trajectory that spans diverse landscapes in the hospitality world. His professional voyage has taken him from the challenging waters of a family-owned river rafting company in the Rocky Mountains to the refined elegance of 5-star luxury resorts, with stops at boutique establishments, country clubs, and sprawling convention resorts along the way. Throughout this remarkable journey, he has not only honed his leadership skills in varied settings but has also effectively managed thousands of employees, further solidifying his reputation as a visionary leader in the industry.

Kevin's exceptional breadth of experience is a beacon for both emerging and seasoned leaders. His impressive resume spans the multifaceted domains of the industry, including property operations, golf, tennis recreational facilities, room management, sales marketing, accounting, food beverage services, spa operations, and the intricacies of asset management. Through his extensive tenure, he has not only honed his skills but also garnered invaluable insights into the nuances of leadership within diverse departmental environments.

What sets Kevin apart is his strategic acumen, an artistry that has played a pivotal role in shaping property financial strategies, driving capital investments, spearheading membership sales initiatives, and orchestrating owner engagement programs. These endeavors have yielded tangible results, including heightened guest and staff satisfaction, unwavering loyalty, improved profitability, remarkable return on investment, and a consistent enhancement of assets under his purview.

However, Kevin's leadership prowess transcends the boardroom. He epitomizes the highest standards of professional ethics and values, infusing every project with his creative and pragmatic energy. His leadership style revolves around active listening, the seamless integration of groundbreaking ideas, comprehensive education, efficient execution, motivational guidance, empowerment, and a vigorous work ethic. Perhaps most importantly, Kevin prioritizes fostering a vibrant and wholesome work culture where individuals are nurtured to shoulder the responsibility of delivering services of unparalleled quality, innovation, revenue amplification, and cost-effectiveness, perpetually exceeding expectations.

One of Kevin's most significant contributions to the realm of leadership is his vast repository of "Trade Secrets." These invaluable insights, cultivated over his extensive career, are shared generously in his book. As you immerse yourself in its contents, you'll uncover a wealth of wisdom that is certain to enhance your leadership abilities, whether for yourself or your mentees and assist you in shaping your unique leadership brand. This biography serves as a testament to his commitment to leadership excellence and positions him as a revered authority, offering an unparalleled resource for those seeking to elevate their leadership prowess in the ever-evolving landscape of business and talent management.

* * *

Made in the USA
Las Vegas, NV
16 December 2023

82941876R00177